To create the games in this book you will need:

• a computer or laptop with a proper keyboard – an iPad or any other tablet will not work so well.

• an internet connection to download resources used in the book.

It is recommended that children should be supervised when using the internet, especially when using a new website. The publishers and the author cannot be held responsible for the content of the websites referred to in this book.

For further help and resources with this book, visit www.maxw.com or thequestkids.com

The QuestKids® series is an imprint of In Easy Steps Limited
16 Hamilton Terrace, Holly Walk, Leamington Spa,
Warwickshire, United Kingdom CV32 4LY
www.ineasysteps.com
www.thequestkids.com

ISBN: 978-1-84078-957-7

Printed and bound in the United Kingdom

Notice of Liability
Every effort has been made to ensure that this book contains accurate and current information. However, In Easy Steps Limited and the authors shall not be liable for any loss or damage suffered by readers as a result of any information contained herein.

Contributors:
Author: Max Wainewright
Creative Designer: Jo Cowan
Cover & character illustrations: Marcelo (The Bright Agency)

Acknowledgements
The publisher would like to thank iStock for the use of their background illustrations.

Contents

Getting Started

In this book you will learn how to create some amazing graphics using Python. You will also become a great Python coder!

We will start by drawing some simple shapes and learning how to use loops to repeat code. We will discover how random numbers can create elaborate patterns and how to mix colours using variables. Later on in this book we will show you how to draw pictures with code and how to create your own commands by defining your own functions.

Develop your skills and create some amazing graphics!

1 Getting Python

You need to install the Python program on your computer.

Open your web browser and go to **www.python.org**

2 Click Downloads

Click the **Downloads** tab at the top of the page.

Downloads

You can use an iPad app but these instructions are for a desktop or laptop computer.

3 Download Python

Download the latest version of Python for your computer.

Download the latest version fo

Download Python

Looking for Python different OS? Python for Wind macOS, Other

Wait while the file downloads.

4 Run the download

Double-click the downloaded file to start installing the software.

python-3.10.0-....pkg

5 Install the download

Python should now start to install on your computer.

Installing
Python

Follow any steps shown on screen to complete the installation.

Python was designed by Guido van Rossum in the late 1980s.

PYTHON In the real world, Python is used to make website searches work, create games, handle large amounts of data, and create 3D images in movies.

Saying Hello

① Make your first Python file

Start up Python. This launches something called the **shell**. Click **File > New File** to start typing a short file of code.

Python

File   Edit
New File

② Start coding!

Carefully type in the following code:

```
print('Hello')
```

untitled

Hold down the **Shift** key...

SHIFT

...and tap these keys to get the brackets.

(9)   ) 0

The colours of your code change automatically to help you read your code.

③ Save your file

Click **File > Save**.

Save as: hello ←   Sa
📁 Documents
dogs.jpeg

Type in **hello** as the file name.

Browse to your **Documents** folder.

Save   Click **Save**.

④ Run the code

Click **Run > Run Module**.

Run   Options
Run Module
Run Custom

Don't worry if it isn't working yet.

⑤ View your work

When you run some Python code, the results or output from the code appear in the IDLE shell.

```
IDLE shell
>>>
====== RESTART: hello.py ==
Hello
>>>
```

It should look like this.

! Check for errors

If your code doesn't work, go back and check it carefully.

() Make sure you typed the code exactly as shown. Check you have typed the () and ' symbols correctly.

Click **File > Save** and run your code again by repeating Step 4.

USING PYTHON ONLINE

You can use Python online, without installing it on your computer. However, not all online versions let you create graphics. There are also some apps available for the iPad that run Python. If you are using an online Python website you should ignore some steps in the projects in this book — you won't need to save your work or switch on line numbers.

For more information on online Python, visit **maxw.com/pythonlinks**

Giant Circles

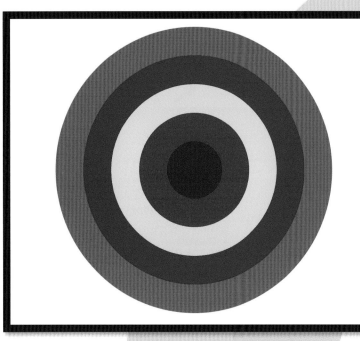

This first project will give you a chance to start coding with Python. We will start by loading the **turtle** commands so that we can do some drawing. This will allow us to type in commands to set the colour and draw some circles. By using different colours and different sized circles we will make some exciting patterns!

HOW THE CODE WORKS

We will start by drawing a very large green circle.	Next, we will draw a large blue circle.	Inside that we will put a medium-sized yellow circle.	A small red circle will be drawn next.	Finally, we will add a very small purple circle.

```
import turtle
```

This tells Python to load some extra commands that will let us draw on the screen. These commands are stored in something called the **turtle module** or **turtle library**.

```
turtle.color('red')
```

This command tells the turtle to draw with red. Make sure you type **color** not **colour**!

```
turtle.dot(500)
```

This will make the turtle draw a dot, 500 pixels wide. The bigger the number, the bigger the dot.

> We'll need to type special commands to draw this pattern.

> A pixel is one of millions of tiny dots on a computer screen that combine together to make images.

1 Make a new Python file

Start up **IDLE** or click **File** > **New File**.

File Edit
New File

2 Switch on the line numbers

Click **Options** > **Show Line Numbers**.

Options Window
Show Code Context
Show Line Numbers

3 Start coding!

Type in your code.

Press the Enter key at the end of each line.

```
1 import turtle        Import the graphics library.
2                      Leave a blank line – it will be clearer to read.
3 turtle.color('green')   Set the green colour.
4 turtle.dot(500)         Draw a very large circle.
```

4 Save your file

Click **File** > **Save**.

Save as: giant
Documents
homework.doc
Save

Type in **giant** as the file name.

Browse to your **Documents** folder.

Click **Save**.

LINE NUMBERS

Line numbers are used in Python to show where an error is. They are also useful for keeping track of where you are when typing in a program.

Don't type in the line numbers – they will show up automatically.

5 Run the code

Click **Run** > **Run Module**.

Run Options
Run Module
Run Custom

F5

Or you can just press the F5 key on the keyboard to run your code.

6 View your work

Your code should make another window appear on your computer.

It should contain a large green circle, like this:

Python Turtle Graphics

! Check for errors

Help!

If you don't get a green circle, go back and check your code carefully.

( ) **'**

Make sure you typed the code exactly as shown. Check you have typed the () and ' symbols correctly.

Finally, click **File** > **Save** and run your code again by repeating Step 5.

→

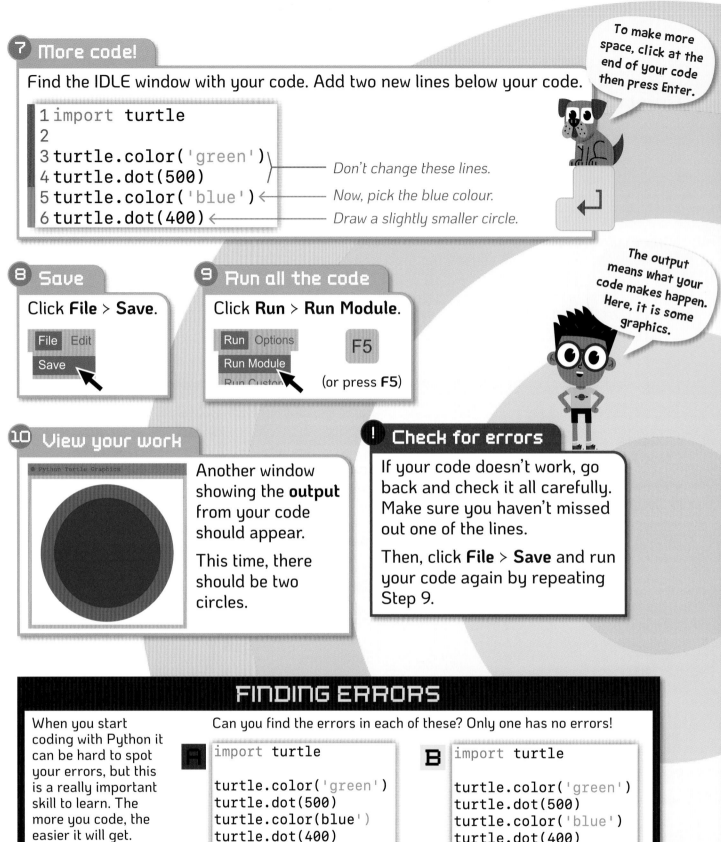

7 More code!

Find the IDLE window with your code. Add two new lines below your code.

```
1 import turtle
2
3 turtle.color('green')
4 turtle.dot(500)
5 turtle.color('blue')
6 turtle.dot(400)
```

Don't change these lines.

Now, pick the blue colour.

Draw a slightly smaller circle.

To make more space, click at the end of your code then press Enter.

8 Save

Click **File** > **Save**.

File   Edit
Save

9 Run all the code

Click **Run** > **Run Module**.

Run   Options
Run Module
Run Custom

F5

(or press **F5**)

The output means what your code makes happen. Here, it is some graphics.

10 View your work

Python Turtle Graphics

Another window showing the **output** from your code should appear.

This time, there should be two circles.

! Check for errors

If your code doesn't work, go back and check it all carefully. Make sure you haven't missed out one of the lines.

Then, click **File** > **Save** and run your code again by repeating Step 9.

FINDING ERRORS

When you start coding with Python it can be hard to spot your errors, but this is a really important skill to learn. The more you code, the easier it will get.

Keep looking up and down your code to look for patterns. IDLE (the Python editor) changes the colour of some code to make it easier for you to find errors.

Can you find the errors in each of these? Only one has no errors!

A
```
import turtle

turtle.color('green')
turtle.dot(500)
turtle.color(blue')
turtle.dot(400)
```

B
```
import turtle

turtle.color('green')
turtle.dot(500)
turtle.color('blue')
turtle.dot(400)
```

C
```
import turtle

turtle.color('green')
turtle.dot(500)
turtle.color'blue')
turtle.dot(400)
```

D
```
impor turtle

turtle.color('green')
turtle.dot(500)
turtle.color('blue')
turtle.dot(400)
```

See below for the answers!

Answers: A) Missing quote mark before blue. B) No errors! C) Missing left bracket after color. D) Import is spelt incorrectly.

8

11 Another circle

Find the IDLE window with your code in. Add the lines of code marked in green (lines 7 to 12).

```
1 import turtle
2
3 turtle.color('green')        Don't change
4 turtle.dot(500)              this part.
5 turtle.color('blue')
6 turtle.dot(400)
7 turtle.color('yellow')  ← Pick yellow.
8 turtle.dot(300)  ← Draw a medium circle.
9 turtle.color('red')  ← Choose red.
10 turtle.dot(200)  ← Draw a smaller circle.
11 turtle.color('purple')  ← Pick purple.
12 turtle.dot(100)  ← Draw a small circle.
```

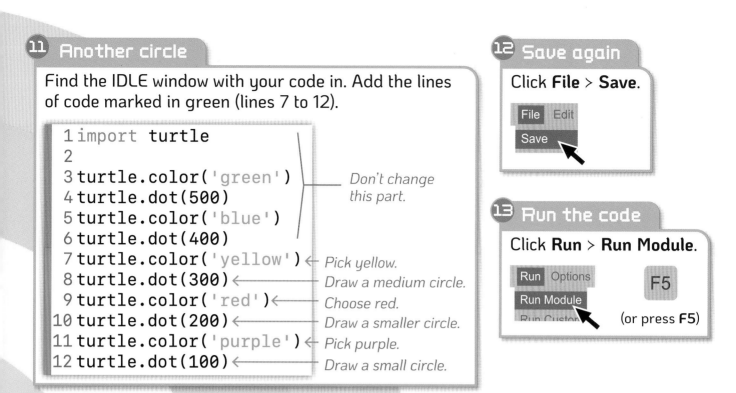

12 Save again

Click **File > Save**.

13 Run the code

Click **Run > Run Module**.

F5

(or press **F5**)

14 View your work

The turtle graphics window should appear with an image like this:

! Check for errors

Check your code carefully if it doesn't work properly. Make sure your follow the pattern of changing colour then drawing a dot on the next line.

After that, save and run your code again.

Challenges

Experiment with your code and make your own designs!

Can you make the following patterns?

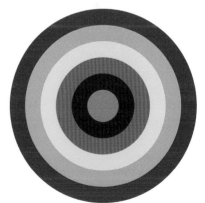

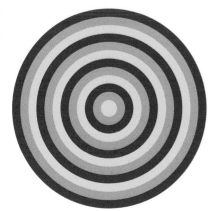

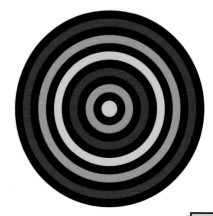

Simple Squares

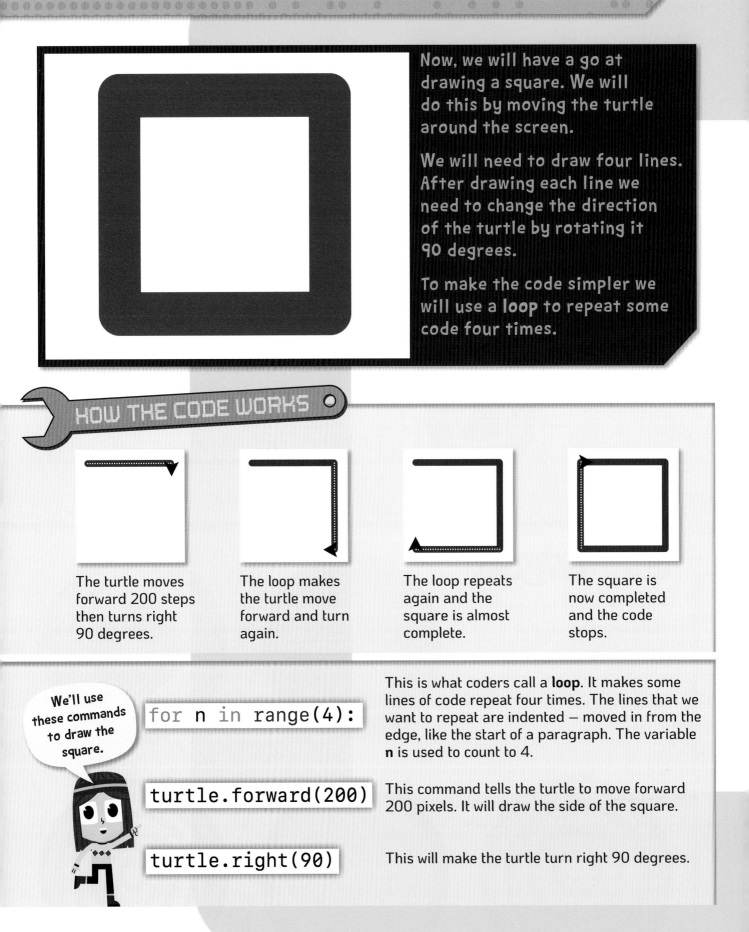

Now, we will have a go at drawing a square. We will do this by moving the turtle around the screen.

We will need to draw four lines. After drawing each line we need to change the direction of the turtle by rotating it 90 degrees.

To make the code simpler we will use a **loop** to repeat some code four times.

HOW THE CODE WORKS

The turtle moves forward 200 steps then turns right 90 degrees.

The loop makes the turtle move forward and turn again.

The loop repeats again and the square is almost complete.

The square is now completed and the code stops.

We'll use these commands to draw the square.

```
for n in range(4):
```

This is what coders call a **loop**. It makes some lines of code repeat four times. The lines that we want to repeat are indented — moved in from the edge, like the start of a paragraph. The variable **n** is used to count to 4.

```
turtle.forward(200)
```

This command tells the turtle to move forward 200 pixels. It will draw the side of the square.

```
turtle.right(90)
```

This will make the turtle turn right 90 degrees.

1 Make a new Python file

Start up **IDLE** or click **File > New File**.

File Edit
New File

2 Switch on the line numbers

Click **Options > Show Line Numbers**.

Options Window
Show Code Context
Show Line Numbers

3 Start coding!

Type in this code to make a square:

```
1 import turtle ←
2 ←
3 turtle.width(20) ←
4 turtle.color('red') ←
5
6 for n in range(4): ←
7     turtle.forward(200) ←
8     turtle.right(90) ←
```

— *Import the graphics commands.*
— *Leave a gap in your code.*
— *Set the thickness of the lines drawn.*
— *Choose the colour of the square.*

— *Repeat the following code four times:*
— *Move forward 200 steps.*
— *Turn right 90 degrees.*

Press Enter twice to leave a gap.

4 Save your file

Click **File > Save**.

Save as: square ←
📁 Documents
dogs.jpeg

Type in **square** as the file name.

Browse to your **Documents** folder.

Save Click **Save**.

5 Run the code

Click **Run > Run Module**.

Run Options
Run Module
Run Custom

F5

(or press **F5**)

6 View your work

Another window will start and show the results of your code.

It should contain a red square, like this:

● Python Turtle Graphics

? Not working?

Go back and look through your code carefully.

Check you have typed the code exactly as above. Make sure the correct lines are indented.

Click **File > Save** and run your code.

Challenges

Change the number 20 in line 3. What happens?

Edit line 7 and use a larger number. How does it change the square?

What happens if you change the number in line 6?

Try using different colours, and experiment.

Wow!

11

Square Patterns

Python is a great coding language for creating patterns. By drawing lots of squares we can make various different designs. Once you have got the hang of this, you can play with the code and experiment, making different-sized and different-coloured pieces of art.

HOW THE CODE WORKS

Our project will use two loops. One loop will draw a square, using the code from the previous project.

The other loop will repeat the first loop, making lots of squares. Each square will be rotated 10 degrees to the right to make the pattern above.

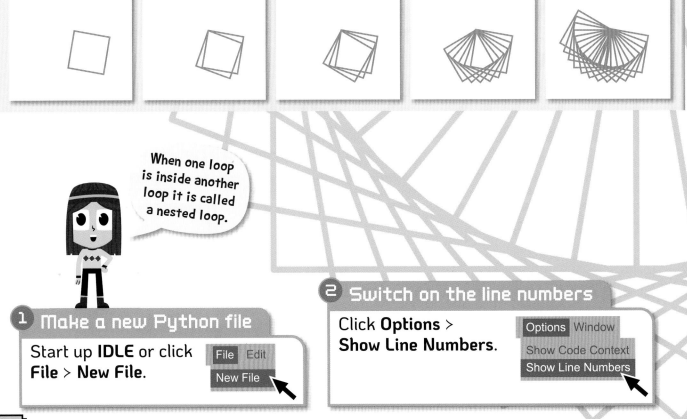

When one loop is inside another loop it is called a nested loop.

1 Make a new Python file

Start up **IDLE** or click **File** > **New File**.

File   Edit
New File

2 Switch on the line numbers

Click **Options** > **Show Line Numbers**.

Options   Window
Show Code Context
Show Line Numbers

I wish I were a turtle...

3 Start coding!

Type in the code below to create a pattern:

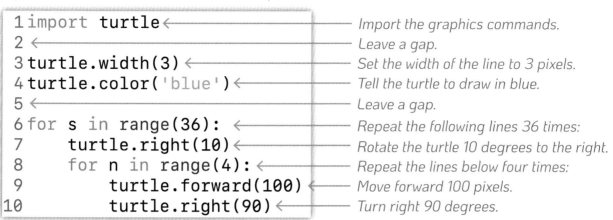

```
1 import turtle          ← Import the graphics commands.
2                        ← Leave a gap.
3 turtle.width(3)        ← Set the width of the line to 3 pixels.
4 turtle.color('blue')   ← Tell the turtle to draw in blue.
5                        ← Leave a gap.
6 for s in range(36):    ← Repeat the following lines 36 times:
7     turtle.right(10)   ← Rotate the turtle 10 degrees to the right.
8     for n in range(4): ← Repeat the lines below four times:
9         turtle.forward(100) ← Move forward 100 pixels.
10        turtle.right(90)    ← Turn right 90 degrees.
```

4 Save your file

Click **File > Save**.

Save as: squares

Documents

dogs.ipeg

Type in **squares** as the file name.

Save Click **Save**.

5 Run the code

Click **Run > Run Module**.

Run Options

Run Module

Run Custom

F5

(or press **F5**)

6 View your work

Another window will start and show the output from your code.

A pattern like this should start to be drawn:

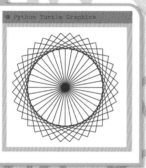

● Python Turtle Graphics

? Having problems?

Check your code carefully.

Make sure you have typed the code exactly as above. Are all the lines indented the right amount?

Click **File > Save** and run your code again.

Challenges

Experiment with colours and line width.

Edit line 9 to make the square bigger or smaller.

In line 6, try changing 36 to 72. Change 10 to 5 in line 7.

INDENTING CODE

Remember — indenting code is very important in Python. The indentations (spaces at the start of a line) are used to tell Python whether lines of code are part of a loop or a section of code.

Python tries to guess when you want to indent some code, but you will have to make some changes yourself. You can always add or delete spaces at the start of a line. Just move your cursor to the start of a line and press the **Backspace** key or the **Space** bar.

Multi Patterns

In this project, the code from the previous activity is used multiple times. This allows us to build up a more complex and interesting pattern. Each block of code draws a square of a different size and colour.

Other effects can be made by using the same-sized square but making the squares thinner in each part of the pattern.

HOW THE CODE WORKS

This pattern is created by running multiple versions of the code from page 15.

The code starts with a pattern made from a red square, 200 pixels in size.

More code draws another pattern on top of it, built with an orange square of 160 pixels.

Finally, a yellow pattern is drawn on top. The square is just 120 pixels in size.

2 Show the line numbers

Click **Options** > **Show Line Numbers**.

Options	Window
Show Code Context	
Show Line Numbers	

1 Make a new Python file

Start up **IDLE** or click **File** > **New File**.

File	Edit
New File	

SAME SIZE, DIFFERENT WIDTH AND COLOUR

Draw a black square 200 pixels in size, with a line width of 30 pixels.

Next, draw a gold square 200 pixels in size, but set its width to 10 pixels.

Nice!

Type in the code below to create a pattern:

```
1 import turtle
2 turtle.speed(0)
3
4 turtle.width(4)
5 turtle.color('red')
6 for s in range(36):
7     turtle.right(10)
8     for n in range(4):
9         turtle.forward(200)
10        turtle.right(90)
11
12 turtle.width(4)
13 turtle.color('orange')
14 for s in range(36):
15     turtle.right(10)
16     for n in range(4):
17         turtle.forward(160)
18         turtle.right(90)
```

Import the graphics module.
Set the turtle's speed to fast.

Set the line width to 4 pixels.
Choose the colour red to draw with.
Repeat the following lines 36 times:
Rotate the turtle 10 degrees to the right.
Repeat the lines below four times:
Move forward 200 pixels.
Turn right 90 degrees.

Keep the line width at 4 pixels.
Now, draw in orange.
Repeat the following lines 36 times:
Rotate the turtle 10 degrees to the right.
Repeat the lines below four times:
Move forward 160 pixels.
Turn right 90 degrees.

Make sure all your code is indented correctly.

4 Save your file

Click **File** > **Save**.

Save as: multi

Documents

Type in **multi** as the file name.

Save Click **Save**.

5 Run the code

Click **Run** > **Run Module**.

Run Options
Run Module
Run Custom

F5

(or press **F5**)

6 View your work

Python Turtle Graphics

The graphics window will appear and show the first two parts of the pattern.

? Having problems?

Go through your code carefully.

Check you have entered the code exactly as above. Are all the lines indented the right amount?

Once you have the first two patterns working, try to add the third one yourself!

Challenges

Try to make some of these patterns:

Spinning Circles

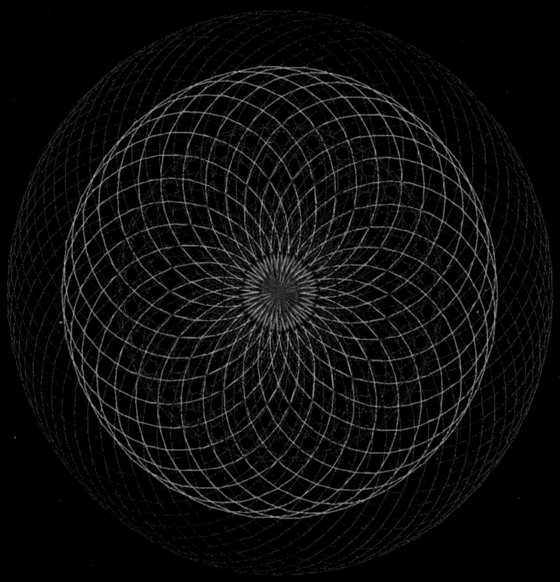

We can make a filled circle in Python by using the dot command. To make an unfilled circle, we need to adapt the code we used to make a square. Instead of drawing a shape with four sides, we will draw one with 36 sides – which will look like a circle. By drawing lots of rotated circles, we can create an amazing pattern!

A square has four sides. The turtle turns 90 degrees at each corner.

To make our "circle" we will just turn 10 degrees after each line.

36 x 10 = 360

HOW THE CODE WORKS

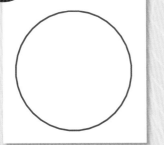

Although this looks like a circle, it is in fact drawn with straight lines.

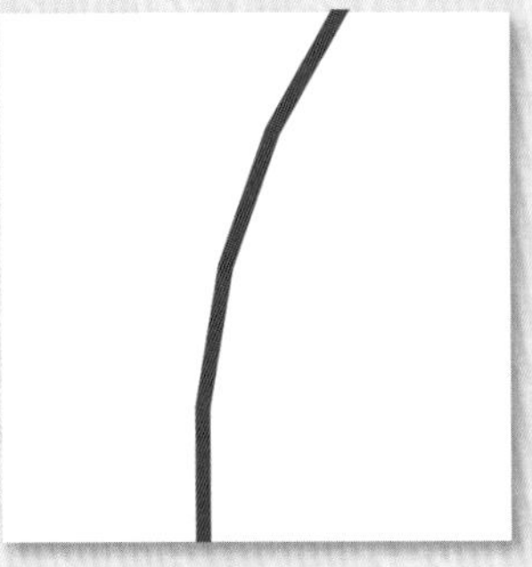

If we zoom in enough we can see it is really a polygon shape. It has 36 sides.

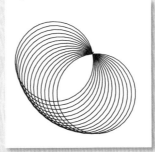

Our pattern is created by drawing a "circle" then rotating the turtle 6 degrees and drawing another circle.

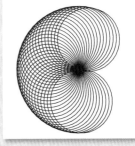

Gradually, the pattern is built up as more and more "circles" are drawn.

1 Make a new Python file

Start up **IDLE** or click **File > New File**.

File   Edit
New File

2 Show the line numbers

Click **Options > Show Line Numbers**.

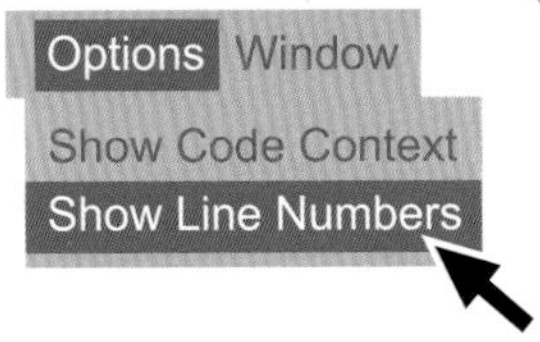

Options Window
Show Code Context
Show Line Numbers

3 Start coding!

Type in this code to make a square:

```
1  import turtle              ← Import the graphics module.
2  turtle.speed(0)            ← Set the speed of the turtle to fast.
3  turtle.bgcolor('black')    ← Colour the background in black.
4
5  turtle.color('red')        ← Draw in red.
6  for c in range(60):        ← Repeat the following code 60 times:
7      for n in range(36):    ← Repeat the next two lines 36 times:
8          turtle.fd(25)      ← Move forward 25 pixels.
9          turtle.rt(10)      ← Turn right 10 degrees.
10     turtle.rt(6)           ← Turn right 6 degrees.
11
12 turtle.color('gold')       ← Now, draw in gold.
13 for c in range(30):        ← Repeat the following code 30 times:
14     for n in range(36):    ← Repeat the next two lines 36 times:
15         turtle.fd(20)      ← Move forward 20 pixels.
16         turtle.rt(10)      ← Turn right 10 degrees.
17     turtle.rt(12)          ← Turn right 12 degrees.
```

> Take care with the indentation of each line so that Python knows which parts to repeat.

4 Save your file

Click **File** > **Save**.

Save as: circles ←

Documents

dogs.jpeg

Type in **circles** as the file name.

Save Click **Save**.

5 Run the code

Click **Run** > **Run Module**.

Run Options
Run Module
Run Custom

F5

(or press **F5**)

6 See the circles!

A new window will pop up and show the results of your code.

It should look like this:

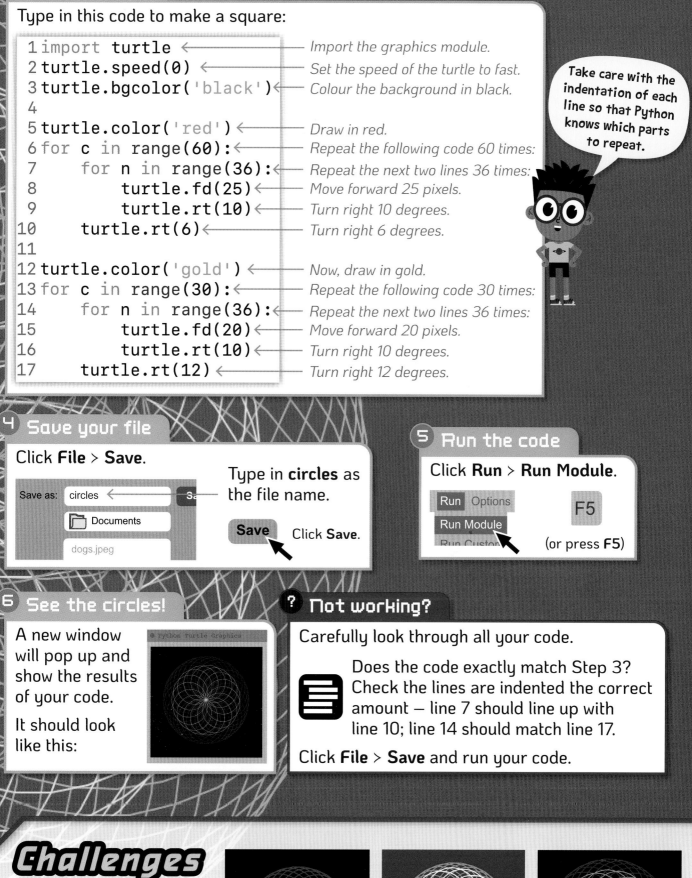

? Not working?

Carefully look through all your code.

Does the code exactly match Step 3? Check the lines are indented the correct amount — line 7 should line up with line 10; line 14 should match line 17.

Click **File** > **Save** and run your code.

Challenges

Experiment with colours and how far the turtle moves forward. Can you make these patterns?

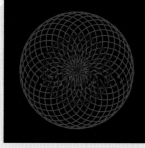

A BIT RANDOM

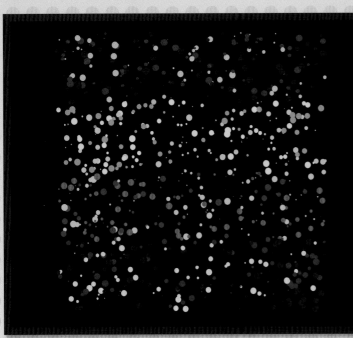

All the patterns in this next section of the book are made by using a loop to draw something over and over again.

We can use this approach to draw hundreds or even thousands of dots or lines.

But to make this interesting, we will need to make each dot or line different. To do this, we will need some new code – the **random** module.

Using the random module

To use any of the commands in the **random** module we need to load it first.

```
import random
```

This tells Python to import (load) all the commands to do with making things random.

We have already used import to load the turtle module.

A module (or library) is a group of commands that do related things.

Picking a random number

Throwing a dice gives us a random number between 1 and 6. We can do this with code using the **randint** command.

```
random.randint(1,6)
```

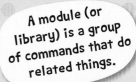

The smallest number to pick.

The largest number to pick.

randint is short for random integer. An integer is a whole number.

Drawing a random-sized dot

To draw a random-sized circle we can use some code, like this:

```
size=random.randint(80,400)
```

Pick a random number between 80 and 400. Store it in a variable called **size**.

```
turtle.dot(size)
```

Draw a dot as big as the value stored in the **size** variable.

Storing the random number in a variable makes it easier to read our code.

Choosing a random colour

We can easily pick a random colour by making a list.

```
paint=['red','blue','pink']
```

Create a list called **paint** with three items.

```
turtle.color(random.choice(paint))
```

Set the turtle colour to one of the items in the list.

Later on in the book we will find how to make random colours in up to 16 million shades!

Moving to a random place

We can easily send the turtle to a random position on the screen.

```
x=random.randint(0,100)
```

Choose a random number between 0 and 100. Store it in a variable called **x**.

```
y=random.randint(0,100)
```

Do the same for **y**.

```
turtle.goto(x,y)
```

Move the turtle to the coordinates (**x,y**).

Making a random decimal

The **randint** command makes integers (whole numbers). If you want to make a decimal you need to use the uniform command.

```
random.uniform(0.5,2.5)
```

The smallest value to pick.

The largest value to pick.

0.98

1.87

0.6

2.452   1.5

2.3

Random Dots

This project will draw a simple pattern made up of randomly-placed dots on the screen. A loop will repeat 10 times, drawing each of the dots. Two variables, x and y, will be used to set the coordinates of each dot. These variables will be given random values whenever the loop runs.

1 Make a new Python file

Start up **IDLE** or click **File > New File**.

File Edit
New File

2 Switch on the line numbers

Click **Options > Show Line Numbers**.

Options Window
Show Code Context
Show Line Numbers

3 Start coding!

Type in this code:

```
1 import turtle          ← Import the graphics commands.
2 import random          ← Import the random library.
3
4 for n in range(10):    ← Repeat the code below 10 times:
5   x=random.randint(0,100)  ← Make a variable called x. Give it a random value between 0 and 100.
6   y=random.randint(0,100)  ← Create another variable called y, with a random value from 0 to 100.
7   turtle.goto(x,y)     ← Move the turtle to the coordinates (x,y).
8   turtle.dot(20)       ← Draw a dot 20 pixels wide.
```

This project uses the random module to pick numbers...

...and the turtle module to turn the numbers into dots on the screen.

4 Save your file

Click **File** > **Save**.

Save as:	random dots ←
	📁 Documents
	dogs.jpeg

Type **random dots** as the file name.

Save Click **Save**.

5 Run the code

Click **Run** > **Run Module**.

Run	Options	F5
Run Module	
Run Custom	(or press **F5**)

6 View your work

Python Turtle Graphics

The graphics window will start and will show the output from your code.

A series of dots should be drawn in the top-right part of the window.

! Check for errors

If this doesn't work then go back and look through your code carefully.

( ) Make sure you have typed the code just as it is written in Step 3. Check that lines 5 to 8 are indented, and you typed the colon : at the end of line 4.

Click **File** > **Save** and run your code.

Challenges

Edit line 4 to increase the number of dots drawn by your code.

Change the size of the dot to make it bigger or smaller.

In line 5, change the range of the random values to 0 to 200.

Try changing the range of y values in line 6.

Make the dots fill the screen by using negative (minus numbers) in the range. For example, change line 5 to say (-200,200) instead of (0,100).

Try to make some of these patterns:

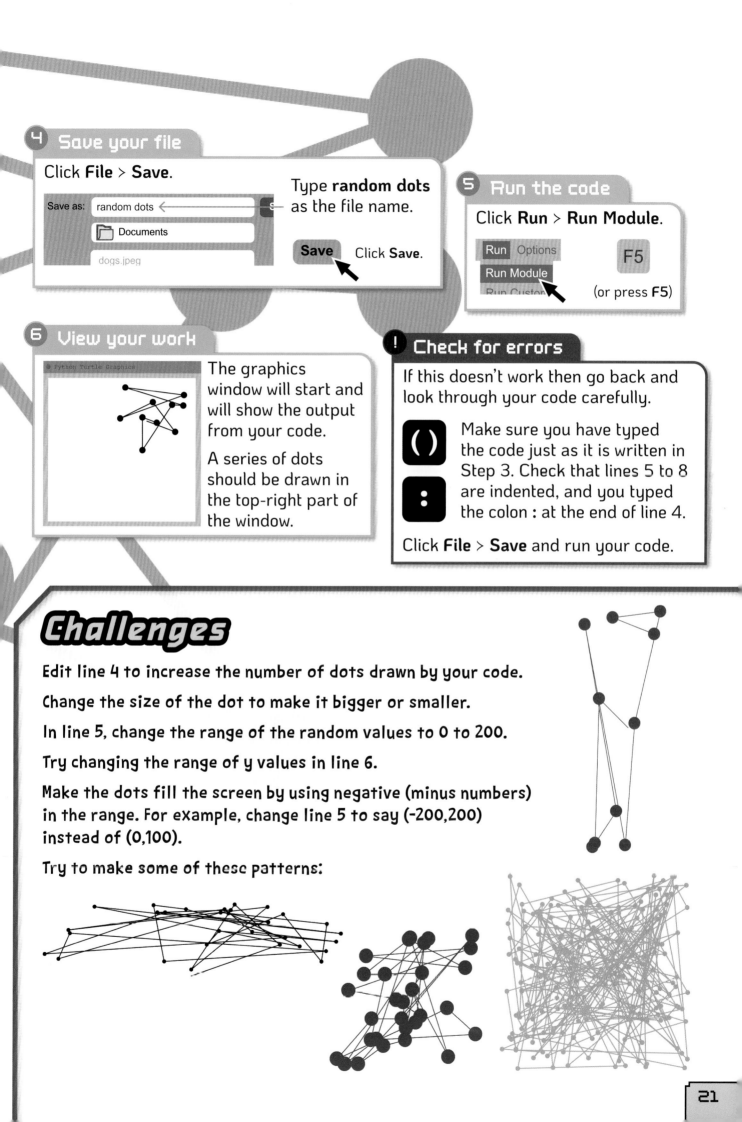

Random Colours

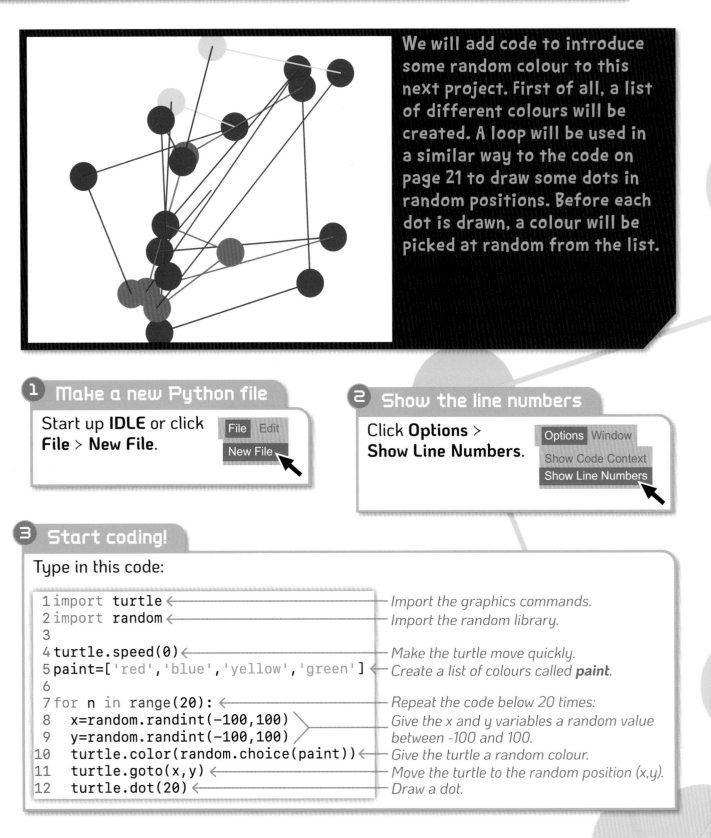

We will add code to introduce some random colour to this next project. First of all, a list of different colours will be created. A loop will be used in a similar way to the code on page 21 to draw some dots in random positions. Before each dot is drawn, a colour will be picked at random from the list.

① Make a new Python file

Start up **IDLE** or click **File > New File**.

| File | Edit |
| New File |

② Show the line numbers

Click **Options > Show Line Numbers**.

| Options | Window |
| Show Code Context |
| Show Line Numbers |

③ Start coding!

Type in this code:

```
1 import turtle
2 import random
3
4 turtle.speed(0)
5 paint=['red','blue','yellow','green']
6
7 for n in range(20):
8   x=random.randint(-100,100)
9   y=random.randint(-100,100)
10   turtle.color(random.choice(paint))
11   turtle.goto(x,y)
12   turtle.dot(20)
```

— Import the graphics commands.
— Import the random library.

— Make the turtle move quickly.
— Create a list of colours called **paint**.

— Repeat the code below 20 times:
Give the x and y variables a random value between -100 and 100.
— Give the turtle a random colour.
— Move the turtle to the random position (x,y).
— Draw a dot.

4 Save your file

Click **File** > **Save**.

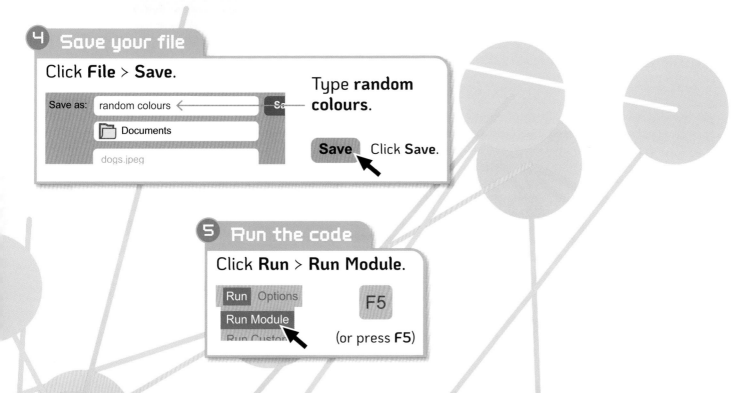

Save as: random colours

Documents

dogs.jpeg

Type **random colours**.

Save   Click **Save**.

5 Run the code

Click **Run** > **Run Module**.

Run Options
Run Module
Run Custom

F5

(or press **F5**)

6 View your work

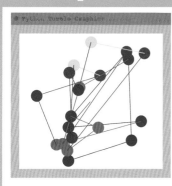

The graphics window will appear and show the output from your code.

20 random coloured dots will show up on the screen.

! Check for errors

If it doesn't work then go back and check your code carefully.

( ) Check you have typed the code just as it is written in Step 3. Make sure lines 8 to 12 are indented.

' Check you have put quote marks around each of the colours in line 5.

Click **File** > **Save** and run your code.

Challenges

Try to make some of these patterns:

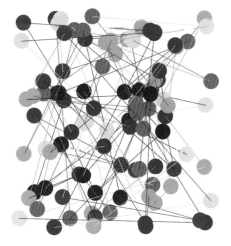

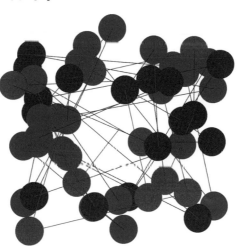

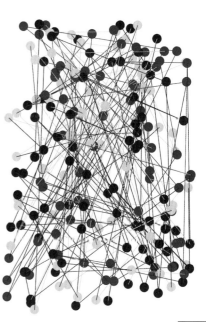

Random Lines

This project will give you another chance to explore random colours, coordinates and loops. We will use similar code to the previous project to move the turtle around the screen. Instead of drawing a dot after moving the turtle, we will just make the line thicker, creating a pattern as it moves.

1 Make a new Python file

Launch **IDLE** or click **File** > **New File**.

File   Edit
New File

2 Show the line numbers

Click **Options** > **Show Line Numbers**.

Options   Window
Show Code Context
Show Line Numbers

3 Start coding!

Type in the following code:

```
1 import turtle
2 import random
3
4 turtle.speed(0)
5 turtle.width(20)
6 paint=['red','blue','yellow','green']
7
8 for n in range(100):
9     x=random.randint(-400,400)
10    y=random.randint(-400,400)
11    turtle.color(random.choice(paint))
12    turtle.goto(x,y)
```

Import the graphics commands.
Import the random library.

Make the turtle move quickly.
Set the line width to 20 pixels.
*Make a list of colours called **paint**.*

Repeat the following lines 100 times:
Give the x and y variables a random value between -400 and 400.
Pick a random colour to draw with.
Draw a line by moving the turtle to a random position (x,y).

We are using a bigger range for x and y, so the design will fill more of the screen.

4 Save your file

Click **File** > **Save**.

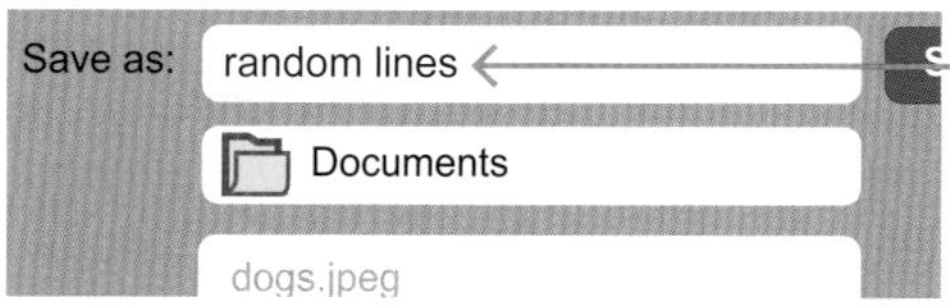

Save as: random lines ←

Documents

dogs.jpeg

Type **random lines** as the file name.

Save Click **Save**.

5 Run the code

Click **Run** > **Run Module**.

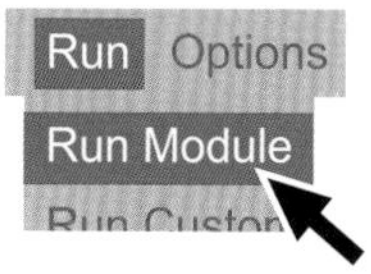

Run | Options
Run Module
Run Custom

F5

(or press **F5**)

6 View your work

The graphics window will show up and display the results of your code.

A series of coloured lines should be drawn in the window.

! Check for errors

If the code doesn't work then go back and look through your code line by line.

( ) Check you have typed the code just as it is written in Step 3. Check that lines 9 to 12 are indented, and you typed the colon : at the end of line 8.

:

Click **File** > **Save** and run your code.

Challenges

Change line 5 to make the line thicker or thinner.

Alter line 8 to increase the number of lines drawn by your code.

Edit the range of the random values for x and y in lines 9 and 10.

Add some additional colours to the list in line 6.

Try to make some of these patterns:

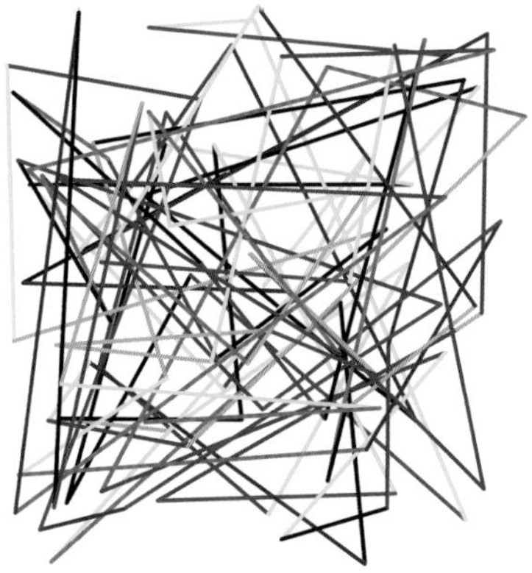

Draw a massive dot at the start of the code to colour the background.

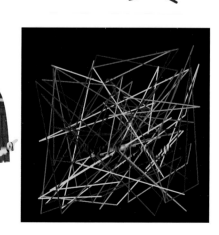

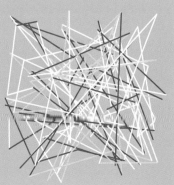

Random Sizes

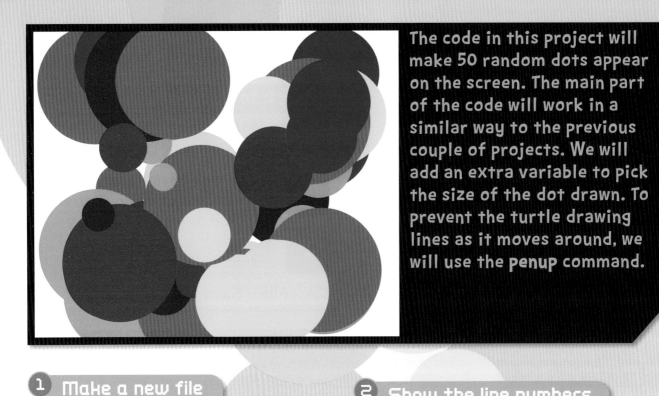

The code in this project will make 50 random dots appear on the screen. The main part of the code will work in a similar way to the previous couple of projects. We will add an extra variable to pick the size of the dot drawn. To prevent the turtle drawing lines as it moves around, we will use the **penup** command.

1 Make a new file

Start up **IDLE** or click **File > New File**.

File   Edit
New File

2 Show the line numbers

Click **Options > Show Line Numbers**.

Options   Window
Show Code Context
Show Line Numbers

3 Start coding!

Type in this code:

```
1 import turtle
2 import random
3
4 turtle.speed(0)
5 turtle.penup()
6 paint=['red','blue','yellow','green']
7
8 for n in range(50):
9     x=random.randint(-400,400)
10    y=random.randint(-400,400)
11    size=random.randint(80,400)
12    turtle.color(random.choice(paint))
13    turtle.goto(x,y)
14    turtle.dot(size)
```

- Import the graphics commands.
- Import the random library.
- Make the turtle move quickly.
- Stop the turtle drawing lines as it moves around.
- Make a list of colours called **paint**.
- Repeat the following code 50 times:
- Give the x and y variables a random value between -400 and 400.
- Pick a random size between 80 and 400.
- Choose a random colour.
- Move to the random position set by x and y.
- Draw a dot as picked by the **size** variable.

Click **File** > **Save**.

Save as: random sizes ⟵

📁 Documents

dogs.jpeg

Type **random sizes** as the file name.

Save Click **Save**.

Click **Run** > **Run Module**.

Run Options
Run Module
Run Custom

F5

(or press **F5**)

● Python Turtle Graphics

The graphics window will launch.

The window should be filled with a collection of random coloured circles.

! Check for errors

If it doesn't work then go back and check your code carefully line by line.

( ) Check you have typed the code exactly as it is written in Step 3. Check that lines 9 to 14 are indented.

: Make sure you have all the brackets correct in line 12.

Click **File** > **Save** then run your code.

Challenges

Experiment with the colours in the **paint** list.

Change the size of the dots by editing the values in line 11.

Try to make some of these patterns:

Edit the values in line 10 to just show dots on part of the screen.

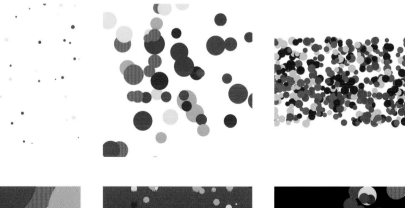

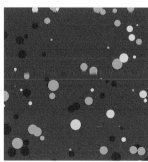

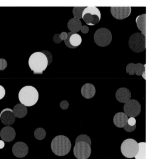

Random Line Burst

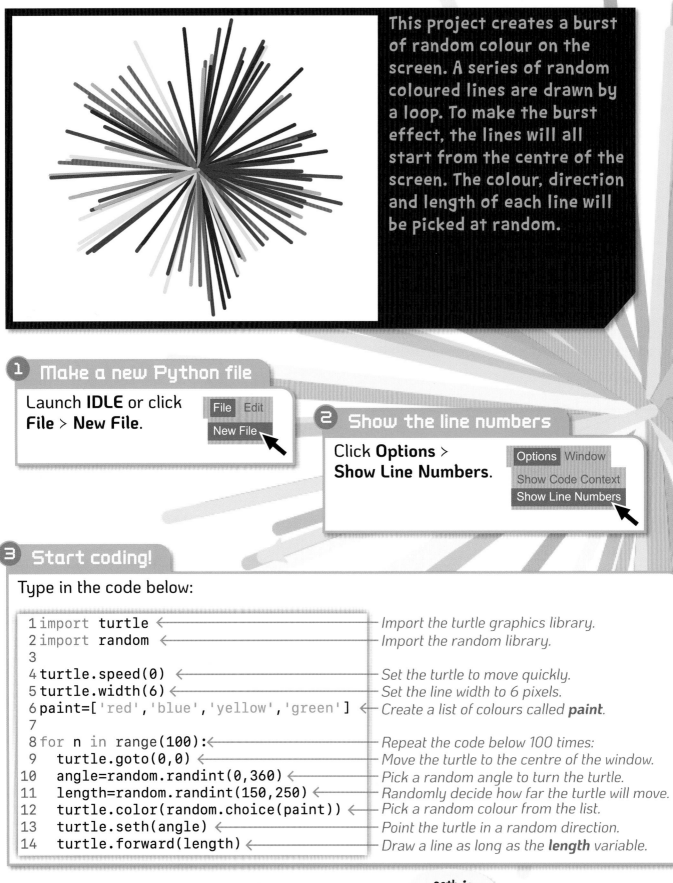

This project creates a burst of random colour on the screen. A series of random coloured lines are drawn by a loop. To make the burst effect, the lines will all start from the centre of the screen. The colour, direction and length of each line will be picked at random.

1 Make a new Python file

Launch **IDLE** or click **File** > **New File**.

File   Edit
New File

2 Show the line numbers

Click **Options** > **Show Line Numbers**.

Options   Window
Show Code Context
Show Line Numbers

3 Start coding!

Type in the code below:

```python
1 import turtle
2 import random
3
4 turtle.speed(0)
5 turtle.width(6)
6 paint=['red','blue','yellow','green']
7
8 for n in range(100):
9     turtle.goto(0,0)
10    angle=random.randint(0,360)
11    length=random.randint(150,250)
12    turtle.color(random.choice(paint))
13    turtle.seth(angle)
14    turtle.forward(length)
```

— Import the turtle graphics library.
— Import the random library.

— Set the turtle to move quickly.
— Set the line width to 6 pixels.
— Create a list of colours called **paint**.

— Repeat the code below 100 times:
— Move the turtle to the centre of the window.
— Pick a random angle to turn the turtle.
— Randomly decide how far the turtle will move.
— Pick a random colour from the list.
— Point the turtle in a random direction.
— Draw a line as long as the **length** variable.

seth is short for set heading.

4 Save your file

Click **File** > **Save**.

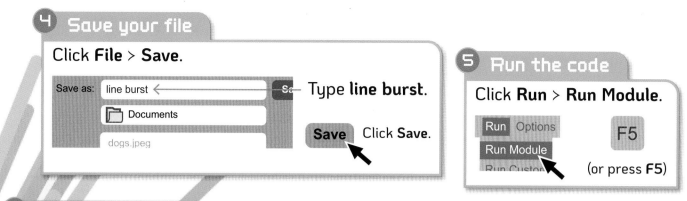

Save as: line burst ← Type **line burst**.

📁 Documents

dogs.jpeg

Save Click **Save**.

5 Run the code

Click **Run** > **Run Module**.

Run	Options
Run Module	
Run Custom	

F5

(or press **F5**)

6 View your work

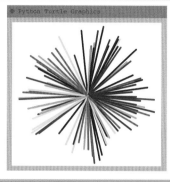

The graphics window should launch and show the output from your code.

Random coloured lines will be drawn on the screen.

! Check for errors

If your code doesn't work then go back and check your code carefully.

 Make sure you have typed the code exactly as it is shown in Step 3. Make sure lines 9 onwards are indented.

Click **File** > **Save** and run your code.

Challenges

Add more colours to the list in line 6.

Try using one colour, but adding "dark" or "light" to the colour – e.g. "dark blue".

Change the loop so that more than 100 lines are drawn.

Make the line thicker or thinner.

Change the angle that is picked so that only numbers between 0 and 180 are chosen.

Alter the length of the line that is drawn by using new values in line 11.

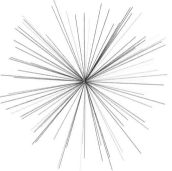

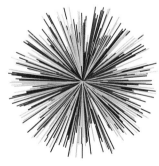

Use turtle.bgcolor at the beginning of the code to colour the background.

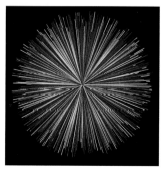

Random Colour Spin

This code in this project creates a similar effect to the code on page 28. But instead of drawing lines at random angles, the **control variable** in the loop sets the direction of each line. As the code runs, colours are picked at random. By moving the turtle a long way, the lines all reach the edge of the screen.

1 Make a new file

Start up **IDLE** or click **File** > **New File**.

File   Edit
New File

2 Show the line numbers

Click **Options** > **Show Line Numbers**.

Options   Window
Show Code Context
Show Line Numbers

3 Start coding!

Type in this code:

```
1 import turtle
2 import random
3
4 turtle.speed(0)
5 turtle.width(120)
6 paint=['red','blue','yellow','green']
7
8 for angle in range(0,360,10):
9    turtle.goto(0,0)
10   turtle.color(random.choice(paint))
11   turtle.seth(angle)
12   turtle.forward(800)
```

— Import the graphics commands.
— Import the random library.
— Make the turtle move quickly.
— Set the turtle to draw a very wide line.
— Make a list of colours called **paint**.
— Make a loop that runs from 0 to 360, in steps of 10.
— Move the turtle to the centre of the screen.
— Choose a random colour.
— Point the turtle to the correct angle.
— Draw a long line to the edge of the window.

This code is making me dizzy...

4 Save your file

Click **File** > **Save**.

Save as: colour spin ⟵

📁 Documents

dogs.jpeg

Save Click **Save**.

Type **colour spin** as the file name.

5 Run the code

Click **Run** > **Run Module**.

Run Options

Run Module

Run Custo...

F5

(or press **F5**)

6 View your work

Python Turtle Graphics

The graphics window will start up on the screen.

Random coloured lines should be drawn as the turtle rotates around.

! Check for errors

Check your code carefully line by line if the code doesn't work correctly.

Make sure you have typed the code just as it is written in Step 3. Check that lines 9 to 12 are indented.

Make sure you have typed all the colour words correctly in line 6.

Click **File** > **Save** then run your code.

Challenges

Type some additional colours in the list in line 6.

Edit the width of the line that is drawn.

Change the coordinates that the line starts at. Instead of using (0,0) try using (150,150).

Colour the background in by adding code before you start the **for** loop.

Try to make some of these patterns:

Add a second loop with a different set of colours to make a double pattern.

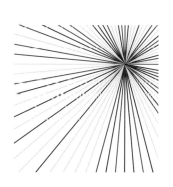

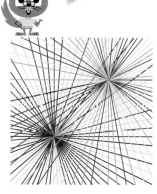

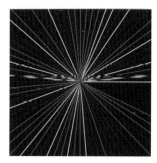

Random Hoops

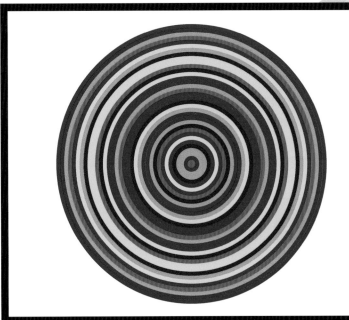

The first project in this book used code to draw a series of dots, creating a coloured target. The code here will automate and randomise that idea. We will use a loop to draw multiple circles, starting with a large circle then another, gradually decreasing in size. The **control** variable from the loop will set the size of the circle. Colours will be picked at random.

HOW THE CODE WORKS

A **for** loop controls this code, using a variable called **size**. This variable starts at 400 and changes its value by -10 each time the loop runs. This makes each dot that it draws get smaller and smaller. A random colour is picked for each of the dots.

 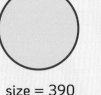

size = 400   size = 390   size = 380   size = 250   size = 10

This looks similar to the Giant Circles activity on Page 8.

But this code uses a loop and random values.

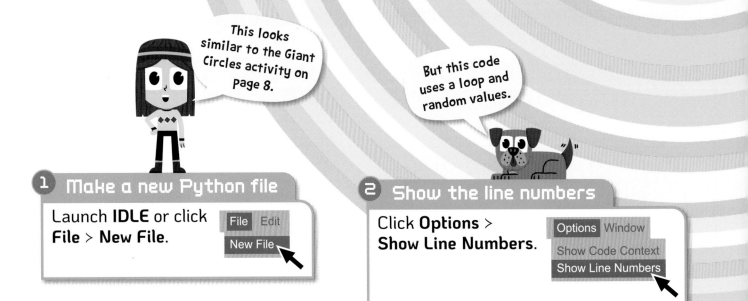

1 Make a new Python file

Launch **IDLE** or click **File > New File**.

File	Edit
New File	

2 Show the line numbers

Click **Options > Show Line Numbers**.

Options	Window
Show Code Context	
Show Line Numbers	

3 Start coding!

Type in this code:

```
1 import turtle ←                                    Import the turtle graphics library.
2 import random ←                                    Import the random library.
3
4 turtle.speed(0) ←                                  Set the turtle to move quickly.
5 paint=['red','blue','yellow','green'] ←           Create a list of colours called paint.
6                                                     Make a loop that runs down from 400 to 0
7 for size in range(400,0,-10): ←                   in steps of negative 10 (-10).
8     turtle.color(random.choice(paint)) ←          Pick a random colour from the list.
9     turtle.dot(size) ←                             Draw a dot the width of the size variable.
```

4 Save your file

Click **File** > **Save**.

Save as: random hoops ←

📁 Documents

dogs.jpeg

Type **random hoops** as the file name.

Save Click **Save**.

5 Run the code

Click **Run** > **Run Module**.

Run Options

Run Module

Run Custom

F5

(or press **F5**)

6 View your work

© Python Turtle Graphics

The graphics window will appear and display the output of your code.

A series of coloured circles should be drawn, getting smaller and smaller.

! Check for errors

If the code doesn't work properly, go back and look through each line of your code.

➕➖ Check you have typed the code just as it is written in Step 3. Make sure you typed -10 (minus 10) in line 7.

Click **File** > **Save** and run your code.

Challenges

Try to make some of these patterns:

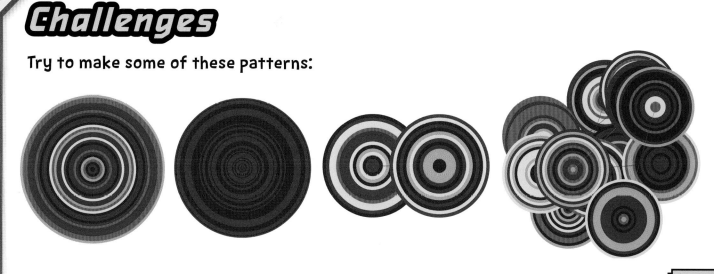

MIXING COLOURS

The projects in the next part of this book explore how colours can be chosen using numbers. Instead of being limited to blue, light blue or dark blue, we can use numbers to specify the shade of blue we want.

By combining this idea with some loops and variables, we will build some amazing patterns using thousands of different shades!

Red, green and blue light

When you are using real paint, mixing red and blue makes purple. Mixing blue and yellow paint makes green.

On a computer we mix light instead of paint. Mixing red and blue light makes purple, but mixing red and green light makes yellow.

By varying the amount of red, blue and green light, we can make any colour.

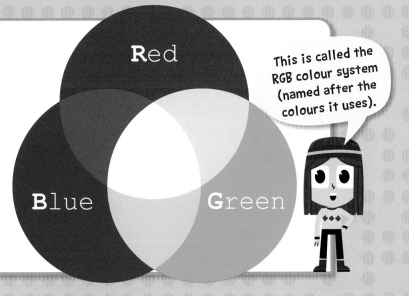

This is called the RGB colour system (named after the colours it uses).

RGB colour modes

We mix a particular colour by specifying the amount of red, green and blue to use.

There are two different ways to say how much of each colour we want:

In this book we will use this mode.

```
turtle.colormode(1.0)
```
The amount of each colour is given as a decimal between 0 and 1.0.

```
turtle.colormode(255)
```
The amount of each colour is given as a number between 0 and 255.

Setting colours

Colours can be set by using the **turtle.color** command, but instead of words we use RGB values.

```
turtle.color(255,0,0)
```
*This sets a colour with maximum red, no green and no blue = **Red**.*

```
turtle.color(0,255,0)
```
*No red, maximum green and no blue = **Green**.*

```
turtle.color(128,0,128)
```
*Medium red, no green and medium blue = **Purple**.*

```
turtle.color(255,255,0)
```
Maximum red and green but no blue = Yellow.

Use this table to make other colours using the RGB system.

COLOUR CODES USING THE RGB SYSTEM

Colour	R	G	B
Red	255	0	0
Orange	255	165	0
Yellow	255	255	0
Green	0	128	0
Blue	0	0	128
Purple	128	0	128
Violet	238	130	238

Colour	R	G	B
Black	0	0	0
Grey	128	128	128
White	255	255	255
Pink	255	192	203
Brown	165	42	42
Dark Blue	0	0	139
Light Blue	173	216	230

Experiment to make other colours, or search for "RGB colour chart" online.

The code will draw a line like this one.

Using code in a loop

We can set the colour to draw with inside a loop.

```
for c in range(255):
    turtle.color(c,0,0)
    turtle.fd(2)
```

Make a loop that runs from 0 to 255.
*Set the colour using the value of the variable **c**.*
Move the turtle forward two steps.

When the loop runs, the control variable **c** will change. This then causes the colour of the line to change too.

There are 256 x 256 x 256 = over 16 million different shades that can be made like this!

Setting a fully-random colour

To pick a fully-random colour, use code like this:

```
r=random.randint(0,255)
g=random.randint(0,255)
b=random.randint(0,255)
turtle.color(r,g,b)
```

*Pick a random number between 0 to 255 and store it in a variable called **r**.*
*Do the same with a variable called **g**.*
*And the same with a variable called **b**.*
Set the turtle's colour using these random values.

Blended Square

We will start off by drawing a simple square. A series of lines will be drawn by the turtle, each one a slightly different colour. The control variable in the loop will be used to set part of the RGB colour value so that the colours gently blend together as the square is drawn.

HOW THE CODE WORKS

A **for** loop controls this code, using a variable called **x**. As **x** grows from 0 to 200, it draws the square one line at a time. The value of **x** is used to mix the line's colour, so each line is a slightly different colour.

 x=0

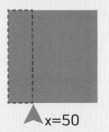 x=50

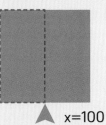 x=100

x=150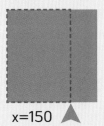

x=200

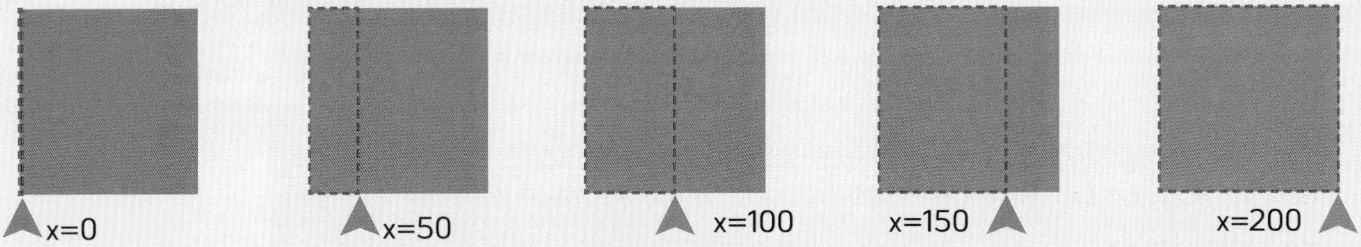

The first line is drawn. The turtle colour (255,128,0) is orange.

More lines have been drawn. The turtle colour (255,128,50) is bright orange.

Half the square is now drawn and the colour (255,128,100) is an orange-pink mix.

The square is nearly finished and the colour (255,128,150) is pink.

The square is complete. The turtle colour (255,128,200) is bright pink.

1 Make a new Python file

Launch **IDLE** or click **File** > **New File**.

File | Edit
New File

2 Show the line numbers

Click **Options** > **Show Line Numbers**.

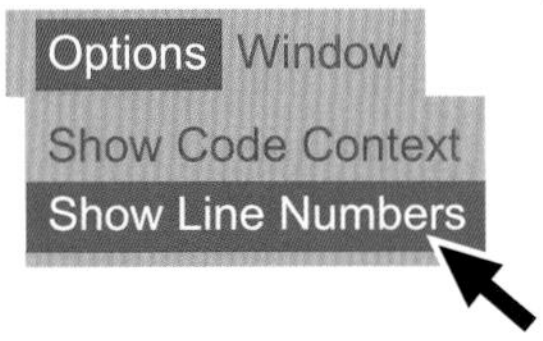

Options | Window
Show Code Context
Show Line Numbers

³ Start coding!

Type the code below into the Python editor:

```
1 import turtle          ← Import the graphics library.
2
3 turtle.speed(0)        ← Tell the turtle to move quickly.
4 turtle.colormode(255)  ← Set the turtle to use colour values from 0 to 255.
5
6 for x in range(0,200): ← Repeat the code below 200 times:
7   turtle.color(255,128,x) ← Set the colour based on the current value of x.
8   turtle.goto(x,0)     ← Gradually move the turtle sideways along the graphics window.
9   turtle.goto(x,200)   ← Draw a line up 200 pixels.
```

⁴ Save your file

Click **File > Save**.

Save as: blended square ←

📁 Documents

dogs.jpeg

Type **blended square** as the file name.

Save Click **Save**.

⁵ Run the code

Click **Run > Run Module**.

Run Options

Run Module

Run Custom

F5

(or press **F5**)

⁶ View your work

The graphics window will show and display the output of your code.

A square like this will be drawn in the top-right part of the window:

Python Turtle Graphics

! Check for errors

If the code doesn't work properly, go back and look through each line of your code.

( ) Check your code matches Step 3. Make sure the brackets and the values are all correct.

Click **File > Save** and run your code.

Challenges

In line 7, try changing 255 to 0 and see what happens.

Change 128 to 0 and run your code to see the effect.

Keep experimenting and try to create some of these squares:

Nice effect!

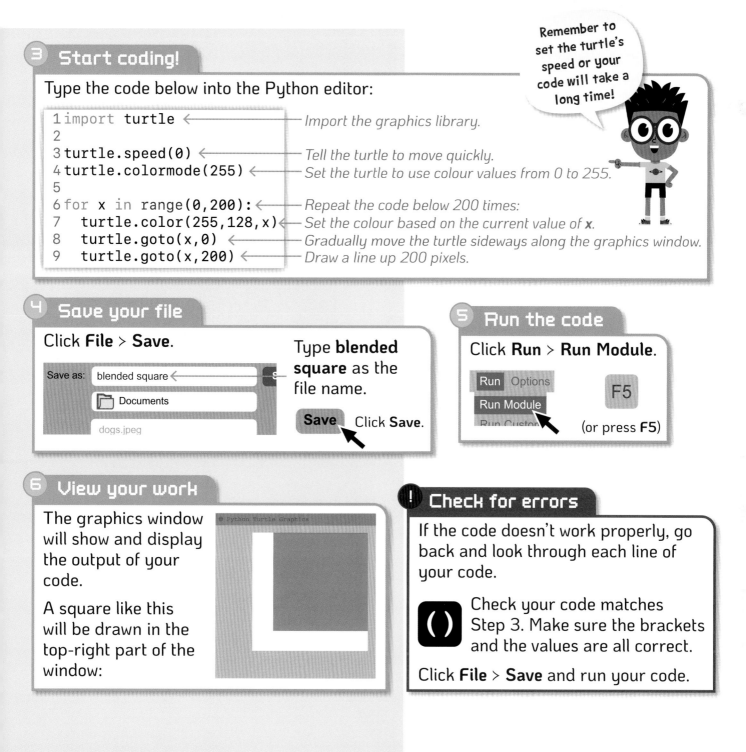

Blended Circle

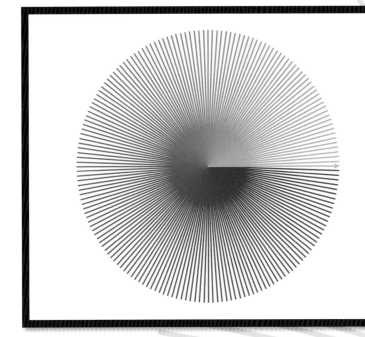

This project shows another way to create a pattern by mixing colours using the RGB system. Multiple lines are drawn from the centre of the graphics window. Each line is a slightly different colour, creating a circular pattern as the code runs.

HOW THE CODE WORKS

Each line is drawn in a slightly different colour. This is because of the **control** variable that counts how many times the loop is run. It also gets used to set the colour of the line. So, each time a new line is drawn, a different value is used to set the colour.

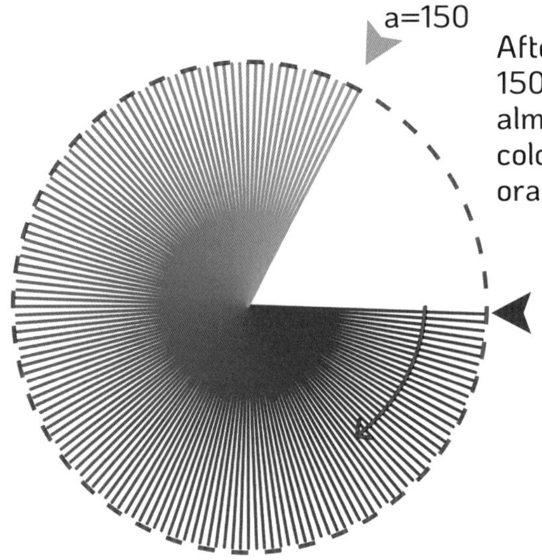

a=150

After the loop has drawn 150 lines, the circle is almost complete. The turtle colour will be (255,150,0) – orange.

a=0

When the line starts, the colour of the turtle will be (255,0,0), which is red.

a=75

By the time this line is drawn, the colour will be (255,75,0) – a mix of red and orange.

1 Make a new Python file

Launch **IDLE** or click **File** > **New File**.

File Edit
New File

2 Show the line numbers

Click **Options** > **Show Line Numbers**.

Options Window
Show Code Context
Show Line Numbers

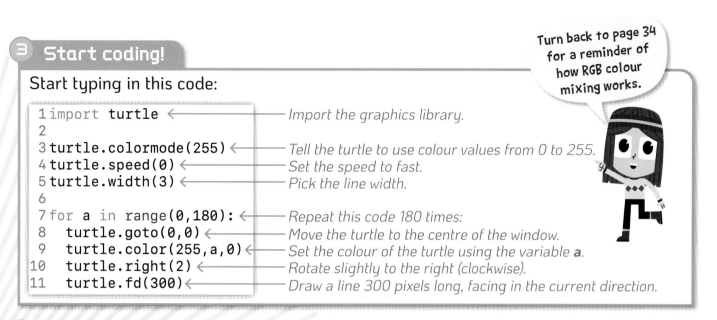

3 Start coding!

Start typing in this code:

Turn back to page 34 for a reminder of how RGB colour mixing works.

```
1 import turtle
2
3 turtle.colormode(255)
4 turtle.speed(0)
5 turtle.width(3)
6
7 for a in range(0,180):
8   turtle.goto(0,0)
9   turtle.color(255,a,0)
10  turtle.right(2)
11  turtle.fd(300)
```

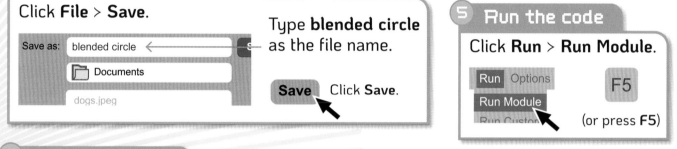

— Import the graphics library.

— Tell the turtle to use colour values from 0 to 255.
— Set the speed to fast.
— Pick the line width.

— Repeat this code 180 times:
— Move the turtle to the centre of the window.
— Set the colour of the turtle using the variable **a**.
— Rotate slightly to the right (clockwise).
— Draw a line 300 pixels long, facing in the current direction.

4 Save your file

Click **File** > **Save**.

Save as: | blended circle
📁 Documents
dogs.jpeg

Type **blended circle** as the file name.

Save Click **Save**.

5 Run the code

Click **Run** > **Run Module**.

Run Options
Run Module
Run Custom

F5

(or press **F5**)

6 View your work

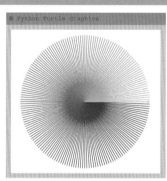

The output from your code will be shown in the graphics window.

A circle should be drawn in the centre of the window.

! Check for errors

If the code doesn't work properly, go back and look through each line of your code.

Check your code against Step 3, making sure all the commands and values are correct.

Click **File** > **Save** and run your code.

Challenges

Use a larger number in line 5 to set the line thickness.

Try rotating by 1 degree instead of 2 in line 10.

Change the amount moved forward from 300 in line 11. What happens to the circle?

Try changing the values in line 9 to (a,255,0) or (128,128,a). Experiment!

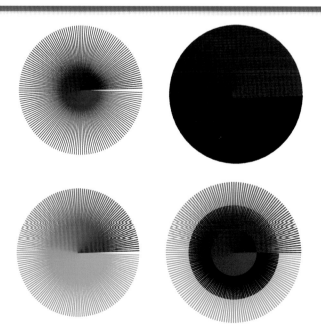

Shaded Sphere

Although this is – strictly speaking – still a circle, the changing colours in this project make it look 3D – more like a sphere. To make the code work we need to run our loop backwards. This means starting with a big number and counting down by –1 (negative 1) each time the loop runs.

HOW THE CODE WORKS

The loop in this code draws 255 circles. It starts with a large circle, then as the loop counts down, each circle becomes slightly smaller. The **size** variable is also used to set the colour of each circle, creating a 3D effect as the colour gradually changes.

size=255

▲ The first circle is drawn. The turtle colour is (255,128,255) – violet.

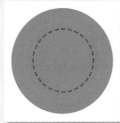

size=165

▲ The 3D effect is starting to show. The colour is (255,128,165) – bright pink.

size=85

▲ The colour becomes coral (255,128,85) as the circles get smaller.

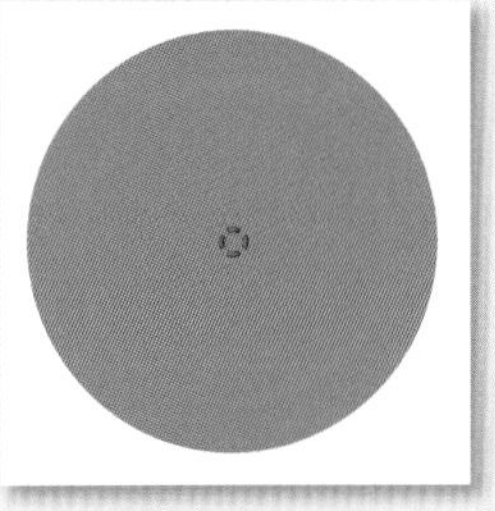

size=1

▲ As the circle becomes a tiny dot, the colour (255,128,1) is a glowing orange.

1 Make a new Python file

Launch **IDLE** or click **File > New File**.

2 Show the line numbers

Click **Options > Show Line Numbers**.

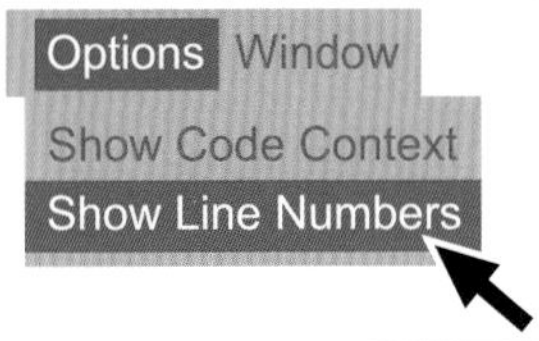

Start coding!

Type the code below into the Python editor:

```
1 import turtle
2
3 turtle.colormode(255)
4 turtle.speed(0)
5
6 for size in range(255,0,-1):
7   turtle.color(255,128,size)
8   turtle.dot(2*size)
```

Import the graphics library.

Use colour values from 0 to 255.
Tell the turtle to move quickly.

Start a loop counting down from 255 to 0.
*Pick a colour to use based on the **size** variable.*
*Draw a dot twice as big as the value of the **size** variable.*

The asterisk * is used to mean multiply in code.

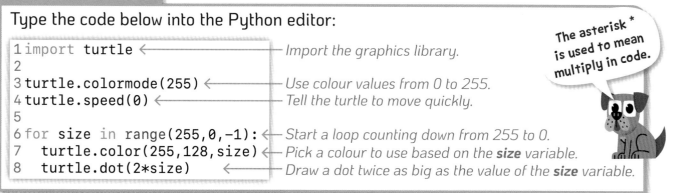

4 Save your file

Click **File** > **Save**.

Save as: sphere

📁 Documents

dogs.jpeg

Type **sphere** as the file name.

Save Click **Save**.

5 Run the code

Click **Run** > **Run Module**.

Run Options

Run Module

Run Custom

F5

(or press **F5**)

6 View your work

A graphics window will pop up and show the output from your code.

A 3D sphere should slowly appear in the window.

! Check for errors

If nothing happens or the code doesn't work properly, go back and check each line of your code.

* Make sure you have typed in all the code correctly. Check you used the asterisk * in line 8.

Click **File** > **Save** and run your code.

Challenges

Wow!

Try changing the values in line 7 to (255,size,0) or (0,128,size).
Keep experimenting and try to make some of these patterns:

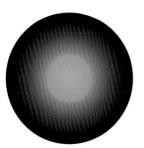

Colour Mix Points

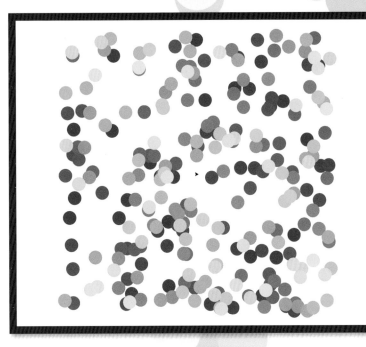

This project will draw hundreds of small dots on the screen. Each one will be positioned in a random place, but they will also be a slightly different colour. A loop will keep the code running. The control variable from the loop will be used to help set the colour, using RGB values.

1 Make a new file

Start up **IDLE** or click **File** > **New File**.

File   Edit
New File

2 Show the line numbers

Click **Options** > **Show Line Numbers**.

Options   Window
Show Code Context
Show Line Numbers

3 Start coding!

Start typing this code into the Python editor:

```
1 import turtle
2 import random
3
4 turtle.penup()
5 turtle.speed(0)
6 turtle.colormode(255)
7
8 for c in range(0,255):
9   x=random.randint(-200,200)
10  y=random.randint(-200,200)
11  turtle.goto(x,y)
12  turtle.color(255,c,0)
13  turtle.dot(20)
```

— Import the turtle graphics commands.
— Import the random library.

— Stop the turtle drawing lines between each dot.
— Set the speed of the turtle to fast.
— Use colour values between 0 and 255.

— Repeat the code below 255 times:
Give the x and y variables a random value between -200 and 200.
— Move the turtle to the coordinates (x,y).
— Set the colour using the variable c.
— Draw a small dot on the screen.

4 Save your file

Click **File** > **Save**.

Save as: points
Documents
dogs.jpeg

Type **points** as the file name.

Save   Click **Save**.

5 Run

Click **Run** > **Run Module**.

Run Options
Run Module
Run Custom

F5

(or press **F5**)

6 View your work

Python Turtle Graphics

The graphics window should show hundreds of coloured dots on the screen.

! Check for errors

If it doesn't work, go back and check each line of code. Click **File** > **Save** and run your code again.

7 More code, more dots

Edit your code to look like this:

```
 8 for c in range(0,255):
 9   for dots in range(5):
10    x=random.randint(-200,200)
11    y=random.randint(-200,200)
12    turtle.goto(x,y)
13    turtle.color(255,c,0)
14    turtle.dot(20)
```

*Click at the end of line 8 and press **Enter** to make space for a new line of code.*

This second loop will repeat all the code below five times.

*Click at the start of line 10 and press the **Tab** key. Make sure all lines from 10 to 14 are indented more than line 9.*

Remember – the indents are an important part of the code.

TAB

8 Save again

Click **File** > **Save**.

File Edit
Save

9 Run the code

Click **Run** > **Run Module**.

Run Options
Run Module
Run Custom

F5

(or press **F5**)

10 View your work

Python Turtle Graphics

The graphics window should now show a lot more dots!

! Check for errors

Make sure that lines 1 to 8 are not indented. Line 9 should be indented and lines 10 to 14 should be double-indented.

Challenges

Try to make some of these patterns:

Spiral Blend

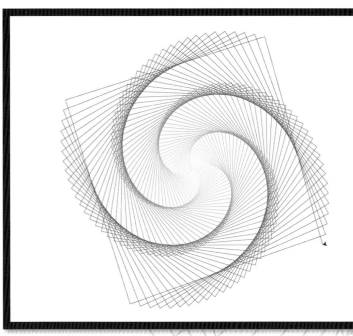

The code in this project will draw a spiral on the screen. Each line in the pattern will be slightly longer and a slightly different colour. We'll start by drawing a spiral based on a square shape, with 90-degree corners. Once this code is working we can adapt it, creating some amazing effects!

1 Make a new Python file

Launch **IDLE** or click **File** > **New File**.

File   Edit

New File

2 Show the line numbers

Click **Options** > **Show Line Numbers**.

Options   Window

Show Code Context

Show Line Numbers

3 Start coding!

Start by typing in this code:

```
1 import turtle
2
3 turtle.speed(0)
4 turtle.colormode(255)
5 turtle.width(1)
6
7 for n in range(255):
8     turtle.pencolor(255,255-n,n)
9     turtle.fd(n*2)
10    turtle.rt(90)
```

— *Import the turtle graphics library.*

— *Set the turtle speed to fast.*
— *Use colour values between 0 and 255.*
— *Choose the line width to draw with.*

— *Repeat the code below 255 times:*
— *Set the turtle colour based on the **n** variable.*
— *Move forward by double the value of **n**.*
— *Turn right 90 degrees.*

4 Save your file

Click **File** > **Save**.

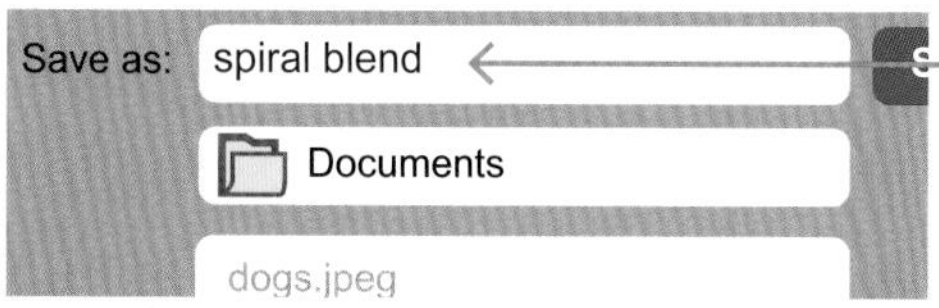

Save as: spiral blend

Documents

dogs.jpeg

Type **spiral blend** as the file name.

Save Click **Save**.

5 Run the code

Click **Run** > **Run Module**.

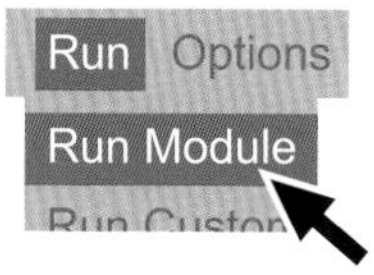

Run Options
Run Module
Run Custom

F5

(or press **F5**)

6 View your work

Python Turtle Graphics

A coloured spiral pattern will appear in the graphics window.

7 One degree more

Edit line 10 of your code to make the turtle turn 91 degrees at each corner instead of 90.

```
10    turtle.rt(91)
```

Turn right 91 degrees.

This change adds a little magic!

! Check for errors

*

If it doesn't work, go back and check each line of code. Click **File** > **Save** and run your code again.

8 Save and run

Save the changes and run your new code.

File Edit
Save

Click **File** > **Save**.

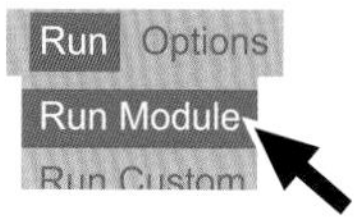

Run Options
Run Module
Run Custom

F5

Click **Run** > **Run Module** or press **F5**.

9 See the changes

Python Turtle Graphics

A new pattern will be drawn in the graphics window.

Try making some of these patterns.

Challenges

In line 10, try turning by 92 or 93 degrees.

What happens if you use n*3 in line 9?

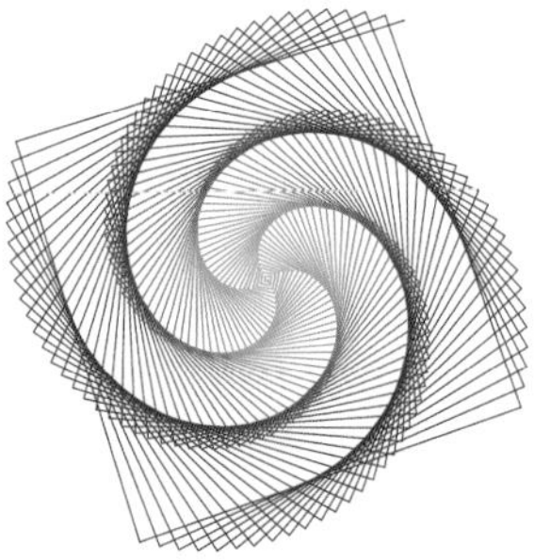

Colour List Spiral

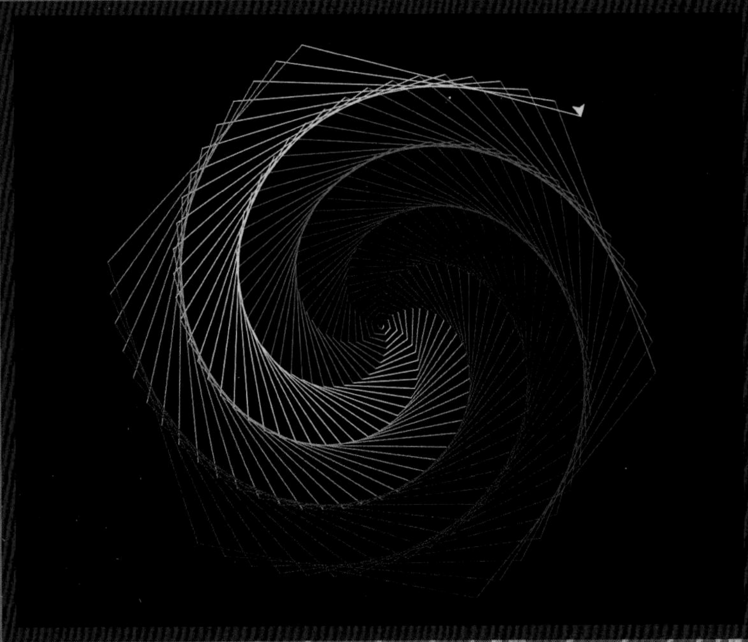

Instead of gradually changing the colour shade, this project uses a different method to choose colours. A spiral is drawn using similar code to the previous activity. Colours are picked in turn from a list of six. Because the spiral being drawn is hexagonal, an interesting colour effect is created.

HOW THE CODE WORKS

A list of colours called **col** is created.

A **for** loop makes the variable **n** increase from 0 up to 254.

A special function works out the remainder when **n** is divided by 6. This function is called **mod** and is represented by the % symbol.

This value, **n%6**, is used to pick a colour from the list, so each colour is used in turn.

A hexagonal spiral is drawn using the colour. Because there are six sides and six colours, this gives us the pattern shown above.

```
col=['red','orange','yellow','green','blue','purple']
```

n	n%6	Colour
0	0	red
1	1	orange
2	2	yellow
3	3	green
4	4	blue
5	5	purple
6	0	red
7	1	orange
8	2	yellow
9	3	green
...and so on...		
253	1	orange
254	2	yellow

The code makes this sequence of colours keep on repeating!

1 Make a new Python file

Launch **IDLE** or click **File > New File**.

> File Edit
> New File

2 Switch on the line numbers

Click **Options > Show Line Numbers**.

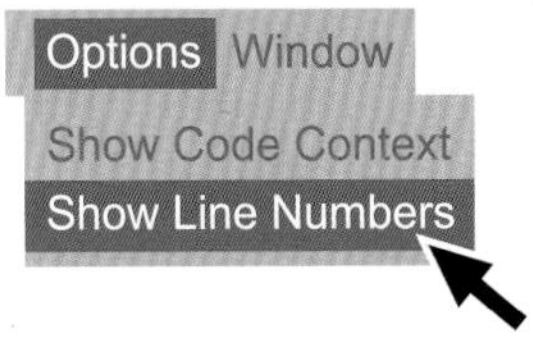

> Options Window
> Show Code Context
> Show Line Numbers

³ Start coding!

Type in this code:

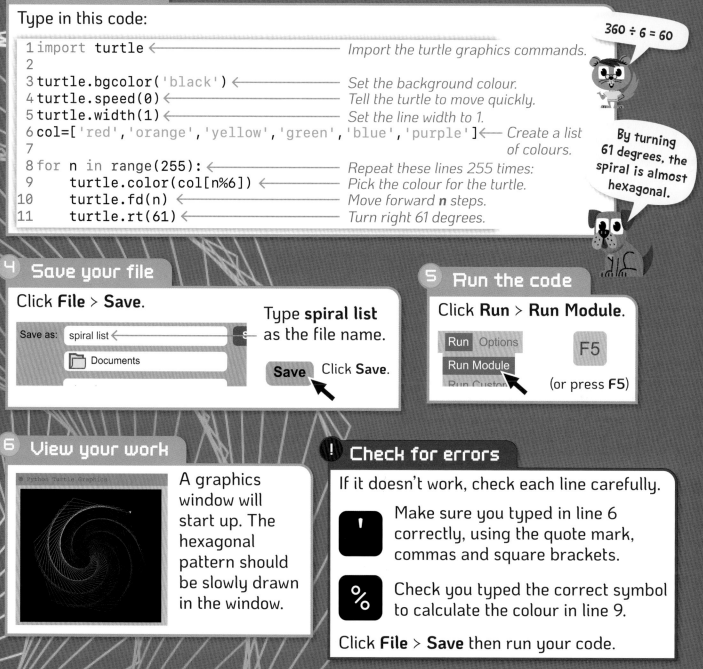

```
1 import turtle
2
3 turtle.bgcolor('black')
4 turtle.speed(0)
5 turtle.width(1)
6 col=['red','orange','yellow','green','blue','purple']
7
8 for n in range(255):
9     turtle.color(col[n%6])
10    turtle.fd(n)
11    turtle.rt(61)
```

Import the turtle graphics commands.

Set the background colour.
Tell the turtle to move quickly.
Set the line width to 1.
Create a list of colours.

Repeat these lines 255 times:
Pick the colour for the turtle.
Move forward **n** steps.
Turn right 61 degrees.

360 ÷ 6 = 60

By turning 61 degrees, the spiral is almost hexagonal.

⁴ Save your file

Click **File** > **Save**.

Save as: spiral list

Documents

Save

Type **spiral list** as the file name.

Click **Save**.

⁵ Run the code

Click **Run** > **Run Module**.

Run   Options
Run Module
Run Custom

F5

(or press **F5**)

⁶ View your work

A graphics window will start up. The hexagonal pattern should be slowly drawn in the window.

! Check for errors

If it doesn't work, check each line carefully.

! Make sure you typed in line 6 correctly, using the quote mark, commas and square brackets.

% Check you typed the correct symbol to calculate the colour in line 9.

Click **File** > **Save** then run your code.

Challenges

Try using a different set of colours in line 6.

Experiment with the angle the turtle turns by in line 11.

DRAWING PICTURES

The next section in this book shows you how to draw pictures using Python. We will use some coding techniques that we've used in the previous projects, such as loops and variables.

Getting things in the right place will become more important, so we will need to be more precise in our use of coordinates to position things.

Planning the picture

If you are going to make your own picture with Python code, you need to plan it carefully. Then, you can start to turn it into code.

Plan the picture in layers, starting with the background.

```
turtle.bgcolor('light blue')
```

Start by drawing a brown dot to be the donut. To get a good colour, we will use RGB values.

```
turtle.color(209,154,98)
turtle.dot(600)
```

Next, we will add some pink icing.

```
turtle.color('pink')
turtle.dot(550)
```

A light blue circle will cut a hole out of the middle of the donut.

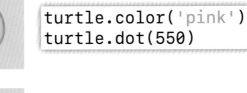

```
turtle.color('light blue')
turtle.dot(220)
```

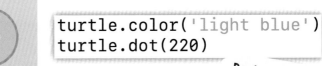

Don't forget to add sprinkles to the donut!

48

Using coordinates

With some pictures, you will need to move the turtle to particular places on the screen.

`turtle.goto(50,60)`

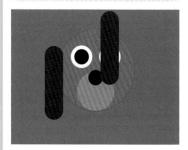

The ear is too far up and too far to the left. We need to make the x value bigger and the y value smaller.

`turtle.goto(110,20)`

Now, the ear is too far to the right! We need to try a value in between the two x values. The y value looks okay.

`turtle.goto(80,20)`

That looks perfect! We have corrected our code using "trial and error".

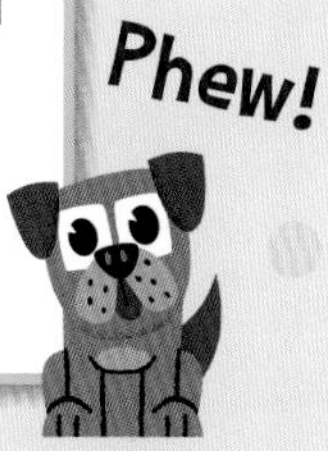

Phew!

Squared paper

Sometimes, it's much easier if you plan out your picture on some squared paper.

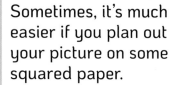

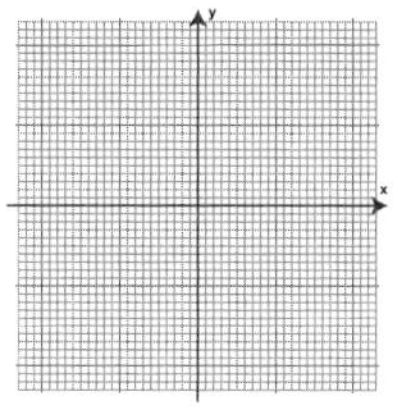

Start by drawing the x and y axes on the paper.

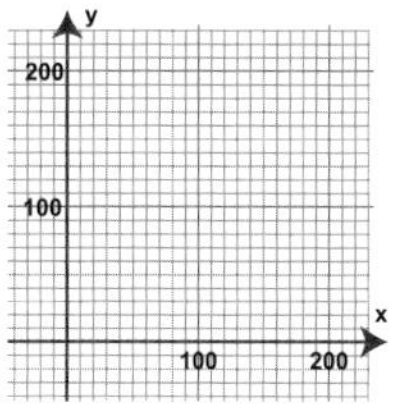

Add numbers to the x and y axes.

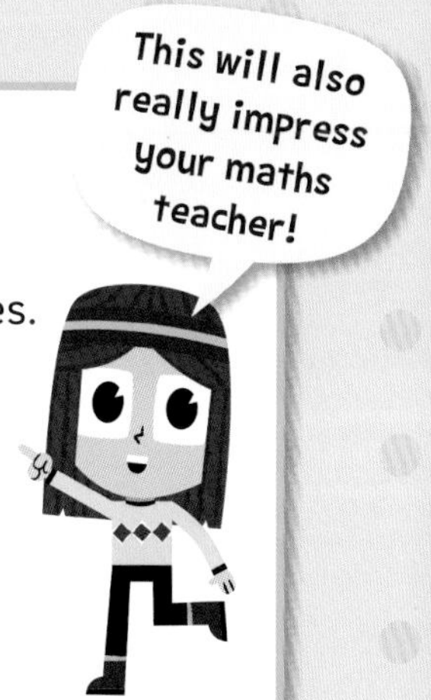

This will also really impress your maths teacher!

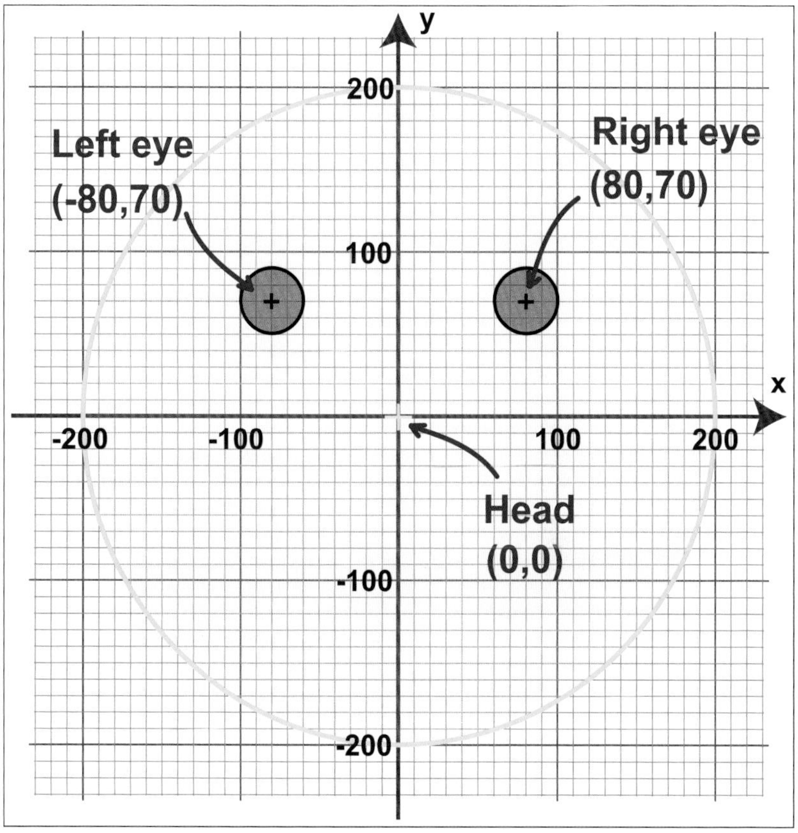

Left eye (-80,70)

Right eye (80,70)

Head (0,0)

Then, you can start planning the code. This will draw a yellow face:

```
turtle.pu()
turtle.color('yellow')
turtle.dot(400)
```

And this will add the right eye:

```
turtle.color('black')
turtle.goto(80,70)
turtle.dot(40)
```

Flower

Our first project in this section is a simple picture of a flower. We will combine together some lines and a dot to make the design. By setting a very wide line width, we will create petals for the flower. A loop will be used to draw five petals in total.

HOW THE CODE WORKS

Point down then draw a green line to be the stem of the flower.

Use a loop to draw a thick orange line for each petal of the flower.

The loop turns 72 degrees each time to make five petals in total.

A red dot in the centre completes the flower.

1 Make a new Python file

Launch **IDLE** or click **File > New File**.

File	Edit
New File	

2 Switch on the line numbers

Click **Options > Show Line Numbers**.

Options	Window
Show Code Context	
Show Line Numbers	

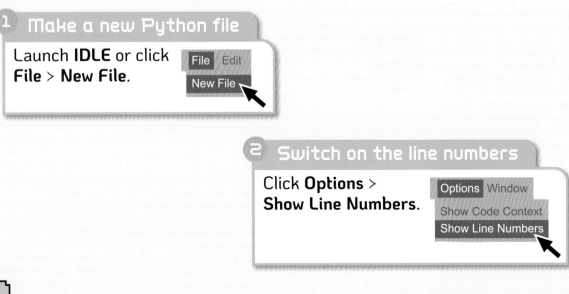

```
 1 import turtle        ←———————————— Import the turtle graphics library.
 2
 3 turtle.width(10)     ←———————————— Set the width to 10 pixels.
 4 turtle.seth(90)      ←———————————— Point the turtle upwards.
 5 turtle.color('green')←———————————— Choose the green colour.
 6 turtle.fd(140)       ←———————————— Draw a line to be the stem of the flower.
 7
 8 for n in range(5):   ←———————————— Repeat the code below five times:
 9     turtle.width(50) ←———————————— Set the width to 50 pixels.
10     turtle.rt(72)    ←———————————— Turn right 72 degrees.
11     turtle.color('orange')←——————— Set the colour to orange.
12     turtle.fd(50)    ←———————————— Move forward to draw the petal.
13     turtle.bk(50)    ←———————————— Move back to the centre.
14
15 turtle.color('red')  ←———————————— Pick a red colour.
16 turtle.dot(60)       ←———————————— Draw the centre of the flower.
```

4 Save your file

Click **File** > **Save**.

Save as: flower ←——
  📁 Documents
  dogs.jpeg

Type **flower** as the file name.

Save Click **Save**.

5 Run the code

Click **Run** > **Run Module**.

Run Options
Run Module
Run Custom

F5

(or press **F5**)

6 View your code

● Python Turtle Graphics

The Turtle Graphics window will appear and your flower will be drawn.

! Check for errors

If this doesn't work then go back and look through your code carefully.

Check your code is exactly as shown above. Make sure lines 9 to 13 are indented.

Click **File** > **Save** and run your code.

Later on in this book we will learn how to make a command to draw a flower.

Challenges

Experiment with different colours for different parts of the flower.

Try making the flower bigger or smaller.

Change the amount the turtle turns in line 10 from 72 to 36. How many times will you need to make the loop repeat in line 8 to complete the flower?

Set the background colour to green.

Pizza

The pizza picture shares some ideas with the donut project. The basic dough, tomato sauce and cheese are drawn by using big circles. Olives will be added on top using a loop. The olives will be placed in random positions. Finally, some lines will be drawn on top to slice up the pizza!

HOW THE CODE WORKS

The background is filled in green.

The code sets the pizza base colour using RGB values.

Tomato sauce is drawn on top with a red dot.

A yellow dot adds cheese to the pizza.

A loop draws 12 black dots on top to show the olives.

A loop draws a green line slice every 45 degrees.

1 Make a new Python file

Start up **IDLE** or click **File > New File**.

File	Edit
New File	

2 Switch on the line numbers

Click **Options > Show Line Numbers**.

Options	Window
Show Code Context	
Show Line Numbers	

```
1 import turtle          ←──────────── Import the turtle graphics library.
2 import random          ←──────────── Import the random commands.
3
4 turtle.colormode(255)  ←──────────── This lets us pick values from 0 to 255 for colours.
5 turtle.bgcolor('light green') ←───── Paint the background light green.
6 turtle.color(220,175,105) ←───────── Set a light brown colour for the pizza base.
7 turtle.dot(600)        ←──────────── Draw the pizza base.
8 turtle.color(220,0,0)  ←──────────── Mix a dark red for the tomato sauce.
9 turtle.dot(500)        ←──────────── Add the sauce to the pizza.
10 turtle.color(255,250,115) ←──────── Pick a yellow colour for the cheese.
11 turtle.dot(465)       ←──────────── Draw the cheese on the pizza.
12
13 turtle.pu()           ←──────────── Stop drawing.
14 for n in range(12):   ←──────────── Repeat the following code 12 times:
15     turtle.goto(0,0)  ←──────────── Move the turtle to the centre.
16     turtle.seth(random.randint(1,360)) ←─Point the turtle in a random direction.
17     turtle.fd(random.randint(50,200)) ←──Move it forward a random amount.
18     turtle.color('black') ←──────── Choose black.
19     turtle.dot(35)    ←──────────── Draw an olive.
20
21 turtle.color('light green') ←─────── Pick the background colour.
22 turtle.width(5)       ←──────────── Set the line width to 5 pixels.
23 for s in range(0,360,45): ←──────── Make a for loop to draw the slice lines.
24     turtle.goto(0,0)  ←──────────── Move to the centre.
25     turtle.pd()       ←──────────── Get ready to draw.
26     turtle.seth(s)    ←──────────── Point the turtle in the correct direction.
27     turtle.fd(300)    ←──────────── Draw a line to slice up the pizza.
```

4 Save your file

Click **File > Save**.

Save as: pizza ←

📁 Documents

dogs.jpeg

Type **pizza** as the file name.

Save Click **Save**.

5 Run the code

Click **Run > Run Module**.

Run Options
Run Module
Run Custom

F5

(or press **F5**)

6 Pizza time

A pizza will be drawn on screen.

! Check for errors

Go back and look through your code carefully.

Did you miss out any lines?

Challenges

Draw green olives instead of black ones.

Change the number of slices.

Add some other toppings to the pizza.

Emojis

It doesn't take a lot of code to draw a simple happy emoji – but everything needs to be in the correct place! We will start by drawing a big yellow circle for the head, then add eyes and a big circle for the mouth. A second yellow circle will be drawn over the top of the mouth, changing it into a smile.

HOW THE CODE WORKS

Draw a big yellow dot to be the face.

Position the turtle using the *goto* command and draw a small black dot.

Draw another small black dot to make the other eye.

Draw a medium-sized black dot to make the mouth.

Draw another yellow dot over the top of the mouth to create a smile.

1 Make a new Python file

Start up **IDLE** or click **File > New File**.

2 Turn on the line numbers

Click **Options > Show Line Numbers**.

turtle.pu() stops it drawing lines but dots will still work.

```
1 import turtle        ──── Import the turtle
2                            graphics library.
3 turtle.pu()         ──── Stop drawing lines.
4 turtle.color('yellow')  ── Set the yellow colour.
5 turtle.dot(400)     ──── Draw a large dot to make the face.
6
7 turtle.color('black')  ── Pick the black colour.
8 turtle.goto(80,70)  ──── Move slightly up and to the right.
9 turtle.dot(40)      ──── Draw the right eye.
10
11 turtle.goto(-80,70)  ──── Move to the left.
12 turtle.dot(40)      ──── Draw the left eye.
13
14 turtle.goto(0,-60)  ──── Move to the centre and down a little.
15 turtle.dot(160)     ──── Draw a medium-sized dot to be the mouth.
16
17 turtle.goto(0,-20)  ──── Position the turtle slightly higher up.
18 turtle.color('yellow')  ── Pick the yellow colour.
19 turtle.dot(180)     ──── Turn the round mouth into a smile.
```

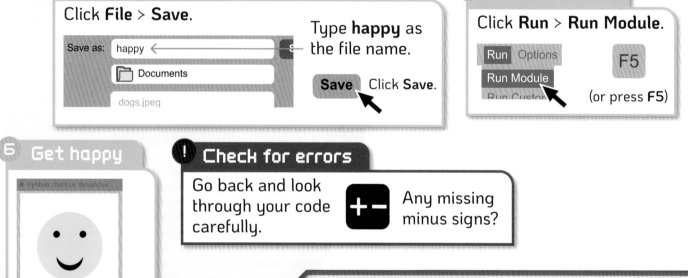

4 Save your file

Click **File** > **Save**.

Save as: happy ←── Type **happy** as the file name.

📁 Documents

Save Click **Save**.

dogs.jpeg

5 Run the code

Click **Run** > **Run Module**.

Run   Options
Run Module
Run Custom

F5

(or press **F5**)

6 Get happy

® Python Turtle Graphics

Your emoji will be drawn on screen.

! Check for errors

Go back and look through your code carefully.

+ - Any missing minus signs?

Challenges

Try making an unhappy emoji. You will need to change the y value in line 17 to -90 or -100.

Improve the unhappy emoji by moving the mouth further down the screen. You will need to change the coordinates of line 14 and line 17 again.

Can you add tears to the emoji?

Edit the code to make an angry red emoji face. Which other emojis can you code?

:) !)

Dog

My fav!

We will start this project by drawing a dog's head. Circles will make its face, eyes and nose. The ears will be drawn with thick lines. Extra code will give it a body, legs and a tail – all made out of lines of various thicknesses. Because this is a long project, we will add comments that will show up in red. This will make the code easier for you to follow.

HOW THE CODE WORKS

Start by setting the background to light blue.

Draw a brown dot to make the dog's head.

Draw a white dot and a smaller black dot to be the left eye.

Move the turtle to the right and draw the right eye.

Set light brown, move down and add a dot to be the muzzle.

Move up a little and add a small black dot to be the nose.

Move left and draw a dark brown line to show the left ear.

Finally, move to the right and draw the right ear.

Click the Options menu and show the line numbers.

1 Make a new file

Start up **IDLE** or click
File > New File.

58

The hash symbol # is used to write comments on a line.

```
 1 import turtle          ←———————————— Import the turtle graphics library.
 2 turtle.pu()            ←———————————— Stop the turtle drawing lines.
 3 turtle.colormode(255)  ←———————————— Set the colour mode to use values from 0 to 255.
 4 #head                  ←———————————— Add a comment in the code to show where the head is drawn.
 5 turtle.color(177,127,74) ← Set the colour for the dog.
 6 turtle.dot(150)        ←———————————— Start by drawing the head.
 7 #left eye              ←———————————— Add a comment to show where the left eye is drawn in the code.
 8 turtle.color('white')  ←———————————— Pick white.
 9 turtle.goto(-30,30)    ←———————————— Move up a little and to the left.
10 turtle.dot(40)         ←———————————— Draw the outer part of the eye.
11 turtle.color('black')  ←———————————— Choose black.
12 turtle.dot(25)         ←———————————— Draw the pupil (the centre of the eye).
13 #right eye             ←———————————— Show where the right eye is drawn in the code.
14 turtle.color('white')  ←———————————— Pick white.
15 turtle.goto(30,30)     ←———————————— Move up a little and to the right.
16 turtle.dot(40)         ←———————————— Draw the outer part of the eye.
17 turtle.color('black')  ←———————————— Choose black.
18 turtle.dot(25)         ←———————————— Draw the pupil.
19 #muzzle                ←———————————— Make a comment that the code draws the muzzle next:
20 turtle.goto(0,-40)     ←———————————— Move to the centre and down a little.
21 turtle.color(202,158,103)← Set a light brown colour.
22 turtle.dot(80)         ←———————————— Draw the dog's muzzle.
23 #nose                  ←———————————— The nose is drawn next.
24 turtle.goto(0,-10)     ←———————————— Move just below the centre.
25 turtle.color('black')  ←———————————— Pick the black colour.
26 turtle.dot(30)         ←———————————— Draw the nose.
27 #left ear              ←———————————— Now, draw the left ear.
28 turtle.width(40)       ←———————————— Set the line width to 40 pixels.
29 turtle.goto(-80,20)    ←———————————— Position the turtle to draw the left ear.
30 turtle.color(104,60,17)← Set the colour to dark brown.
31 turtle.pd()            ←———————————— Get ready to draw.
32 turtle.seth(270)       ←———————————— Point the turtle downwards.
33 turtle.fd(90)          ←———————————— Draw a line to make the left ear.
34 turtle.pu()            ←———————————— Stop drawing again.
35 #right ear             ←———————————— Make a comment to say the right ear is drawn next.
36 turtle.width(40)       ←———————————— Set the line width to 40 pixels.
37 turtle.goto(80,20)     ←———————————— Position the turtle to draw the right ear.
38 turtle.color(104,60,17)← Set the colour to dark brown.
39 turtle.pd()            ←———————————— Get ready to draw again.
40 turtle.seth(270)       ←———————————— Point the turtle down.
41 turtle.fd(90)          ←———————————— Draw a line to make the right ear.
```

The hash sign lets us make comments or notes in our code.

Comments make code much easier to read, fix or change.

Save your file

Click **File** > **Save**.

Save as: dog ⟵
📁 Documents
dogs.jpeg

Type **dog** as the file name.

Save Click **Save**.

4 **Run the code**

Click **Run** > **Run Module**.

Run Options
Run Module
Run Custom

F5

(or press **F5**)

5 **View your work**

The Turtle Graphics window should appear with an image of a dog, like this:

◉ Python Turtle Graphics

! **Check for errors**

If it doesn't work properly, check your code carefully. If things aren't in the correct place, check you haven't left out any minus signs.

Then, save and run your code again.

If the head looks okay then you can try to give the dog a body, legs and a tail.

About time!

Start by drawing a thick line to be the body.

Draw the first leg down to the right.

Add the second back leg.

Make a thinner line to be the dog's tail.

Move the turtle to the front of the body and draw one leg.

Then, finish with the final leg.

We need to draw the body before we draw the head.

6 **Make some space**

Click the cursor at the end of line 1. Press **Enter** a few times to make some space.

```
1 import turtle  ⟵ Press Enter.
2
3
4
5
```

↵

This will give us room to type in the code for the body.

```
 1 import turtle          ←————— Import the turtle graphics library.
 2 #body
 3 turtle.colormode(255)  ←————— Set the colour mode to use values from 0 to 255.
 4 turtle.pu()            ←————— Stop the turtle drawing.
 5 turtle.color(147,96,55) ←———— Set the colour for the dog's body (slightly darker).
 6 turtle.width(150)      ←————— Make the line very wide.
 7 turtle.goto(0,-120)    ←————— Move to just below where the head would be in the middle.
 8 turtle.pd()            ←————— Get the turtle ready to draw.
 9 turtle.goto(350,-120)  ←————— Draw the body across to the right.
10 #back legs
11 turtle.width(60)       ←————— Make the line thinner for the legs.
12 turtle.goto(400,-400)  ←————— Move down to draw the first back leg.
13 turtle.goto(350,-120)  ←————— Move back up to the body.
14 turtle.goto(300,-400)  ←————— Draw the other back leg.
15 #tail
16 turtle.width(20)       ←————— Set the thickness for the tail.
17 turtle.goto(350,-120)  ←————— Move the turtle to where the tail will start on the dog's body.
18 turtle.goto(400,100)   ←————— Draw the tail.
19 turtle.pu()            ←————— Stop the turtle drawing.
20 #front legs
21 turtle.width(60)       ←————— Set the thickness for the legs.
22 turtle.goto(0,-120)    ←————— Move to the front of the body.
23 turtle.pd()            ←————— Make the turtle ready to draw.
24 turtle.goto(-50,-400)  ←————— Draw the first leg.
25 turtle.goto(0,-120)    ←————— Move back up to the body.
26 turtle.goto(50,-400)   ←————— Draw the other front leg.
27 turtle.pu()            ←————— Stop the turtle drawing.
28 turtle.goto(0,0)       ←————— Move the turtle back to where the head will be added.
```

Save the changes and run your new code.

Click **File** > **Save**.　　Click **Run** > **Run Module**
　　　　　　　　　　　　　or press **F5**.

The graphics window should appear again. The dog should now have a body, legs and a tail!

Make some changes to how the dog looks. Change its colour or how long its legs are.

Change where dog is looking by moving the pupils (black circles) to one side.

Give the dog some spots! Can you draw any other animals?

FUNCTIONS

In this section we will look at how we can create our own commands in Python. This is called **creating a function or procedure**.

This makes life much simpler. If you want to draw a flower, you can just type **flower** and one will appear. The catch is, you have to teach Python how to draw a flower first...

Why not just copy and paste?

If you wanted to draw lots of different-sized squares, you could just copy and paste your code over and over again.

← But if you wanted to draw a pattern with 20 different squares, your code could easily be hundreds of lines long!

It's really hard to find a bug in a long piece of code like this one!

Functions use less code

If you made a function to draw a square, your code would be much shorter.

```
15 #head
16 square(0,0,320,'grey')
17 #eyes
18 square(200,180,50,'white')
19 square(210,190,30,'black')
20 square(100,180,50,'white')
21 square(110,190,30,'black')
22 #mouth
```

Functions also make your code much easier to read and fix.

Functions are more flexible

You can make functions do different things, by giving them parameters.

 `flower('red')` `flower('yellow')`

Parameters are a bit like variables.

Defining a function

Before we use a new command, we need to define it.

```
def square():          Start defining the square.
    for n in range(4):     Repeat the following commands four times:
        turtle.fd(200)      Move forward 200 steps.
        turtle.lt(90)       Turn left 90 degrees.
```

def is short for define.

Python will use the definition to draw a square.

Using the function

Just type **square()** to run the new function.

```
square()       Run the function and
               draw a square.
```

This is known as "calling" the function.

Adding a parameter

We can adapt the function so that we can draw a square that is any size!

```
def square(size):          The size parameter
    for n in range(4):      is introduced here...
        turtle.fd(size)      ...and used here.
        turtle.lt(90)
```

To use the function, type a number between the brackets.

```
square(300)
```

300 gets used instead of "size" when the function is used.

RECURSION

Sometimes, functions call themselves. This makes the function run over and over again until something happens, such as one of the parameters getting too small. This is called **recursion**.

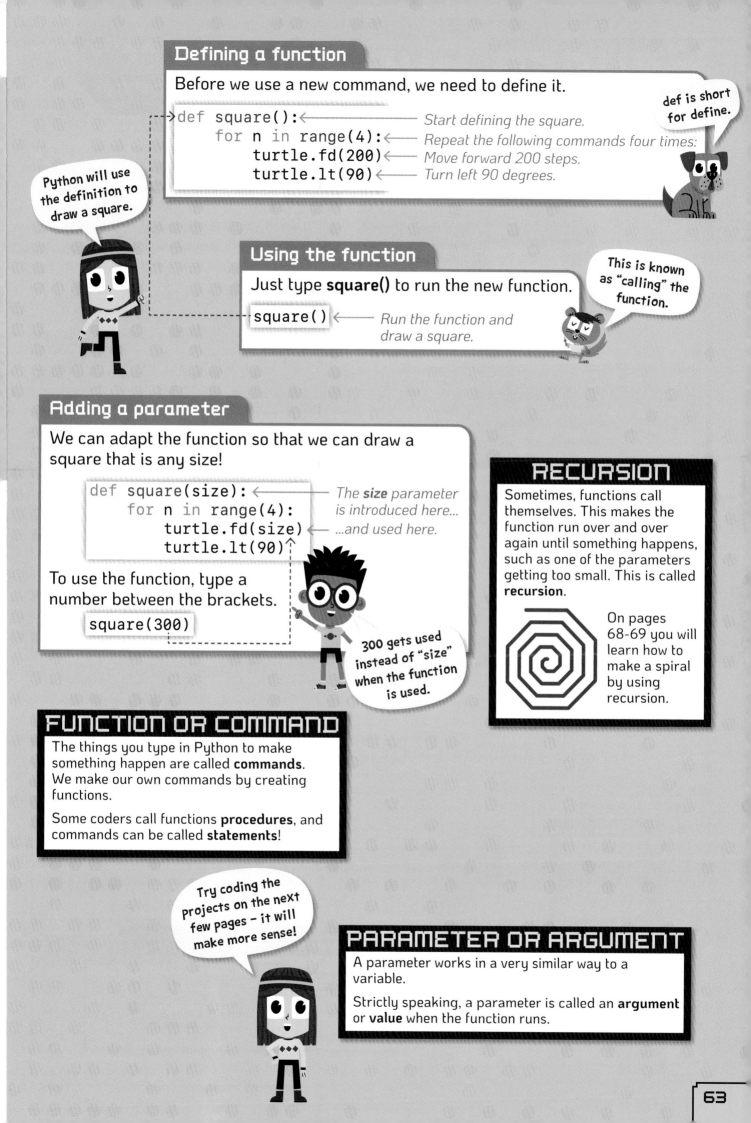

On pages 68-69 you will learn how to make a spiral by using recursion.

FUNCTION OR COMMAND

The things you type in Python to make something happen are called **commands**. We make our own commands by creating functions.

Some coders call functions **procedures**, and commands can be called **statements**!

Try coding the projects on the next few pages – it will make more sense!

PARAMETER OR ARGUMENT

A parameter works in a very similar way to a variable.

Strictly speaking, a parameter is called an **argument** or **value** when the function runs.

Flower Function

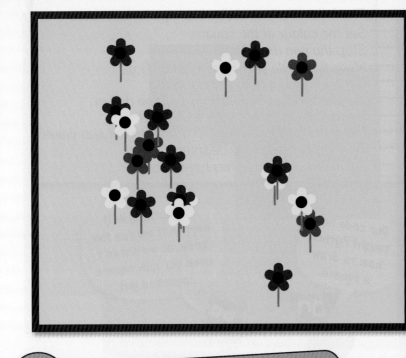

On pages 50-51 we made a simple program to draw one flower. In this project, we will extend this idea and create a function to draw a flower. We will give the function parameters so that we can set each flower's position and colour. Finally, we will add a loop that will use the function to quickly draw 20 randomly-positioned and coloured flowers.

HOW THE CODE WORKS

We will start by making a command to draw a flower.

```
flower(x,y,pCol):
```

Each time we type **flower**, the turtle will draw a flower.

These values will set the **x** and **y** position of the flower.

This value will set the colour of the petals.

Python will look through your code for an explanation of how to draw a flower.

```
def flower(x,y,pCol):
    turtle.pu()
    turtle.goto(x,y)
    turtle.pd()
```

The command **def** will **define** a flower.

Every time the **flower** command is used, Python will use this part of the code to draw the flower.

A loop will keep drawing flowers. Each one will have a random **x** and **y** value to place it in a random place, and be given a random colour from a list.

1 Make a new file

Start up **IDLE** or click **File > New File**.

File	Edit
New File	

2 Show line numbers

Click **Options > Show Line Numbers**.

Options	Window
Show Code Context	
Show Line Numbers	

③ Start coding!

Type in this code:

```
1 import turtle
2 import random
3
4 def flower(x,y,pCol):
5     turtle.pu()
6     turtle.goto(x,y)
7     turtle.pd()
8     turtle.width(5)
9     turtle.seth(90)
10    turtle.color('green')
11    turtle.fd(70)
12
13    for n in range(5):
14        turtle.width(25)
15        turtle.rt(72)
16        turtle.color(pCol)
17        turtle.fd(25)
18        turtle.bk(25)
19    turtle.color('black')
20    turtle.dot(30)
21
22 turtle.speed(0)
23 turtle.bgcolor('lightgreen')
24 cols=['red','purple','yellow']
25
26 for f in range(20):
27    x=random.randint(-300,300)
28    y=random.randint(-300,300)
29    flower(x,y,random.choice(cols))
```

Import the turtle graphics library.
Import the random commands.

Define the flower command.
Lift the turtle up so that it stops drawing.
Move to the coordinates (x,y).
Put the turtle down, ready to draw.
Set the line width to 5.
Point towards the top of the screen.
Choose green to draw the stem.
Draw a line to be the flower's stem.

Make a loop that runs five times.
Set the line width to 25.
Turn right 72 degrees.
Set the petal colour using **pCol**.
Draw one petal.
Move back to the centre of the flower.
Pick the black colour.
Draw the centre of the flower.

Set the turtle's speed to fast.
Draw a light green background.
Make a list of colours for the petals.

Repeat these lines 20 times:
Pick a random x and y value
between -300 and 300.
Draw a random flower.

> The indentation at the start of each line is very important in this project.

> Turn 72 degrees for each of the five petals, because 72 x 5 makes 360 degrees.

④ Save your file

Click **File > Save**.

Save as: flowers
📁 Documents
dogs.jpeg

Type **flowers** as the file name.

Save Click **Save**.

⑤ Run the code

Click **Run > Run Module**.

Run Options
Run Module
Run Custom

F5

(or press **F5**)

⑥ Flowers!

● Python Turtle Graphics

Your screen should start to fill up with random flowers!

⚠ Check for errors

Go back and look through your code carefully. Pay close attention to the indentation of each line.

Challenges

Change line 26 to draw more flowers.

Add extra colours to the list.

Change the number of petals on each flower. You will need to change the amount the turtle rotates in line 15 too.

Make each flower a random size.

Recursive Spiral

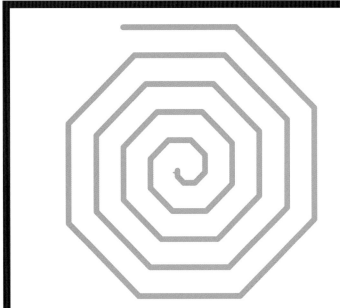

We could draw a spiral by using a loop and a variable. In this project we will use an alternative called **recursion**. This is a way of making a function "call" (run) itself until a task is complete. Here, we will make a function that draws a line then turns 45 degrees. If the line length is more than 10, the function then calls itself to run again, with a shorter side length. This way, a spiral is drawn.

HOW THE CODE WORKS

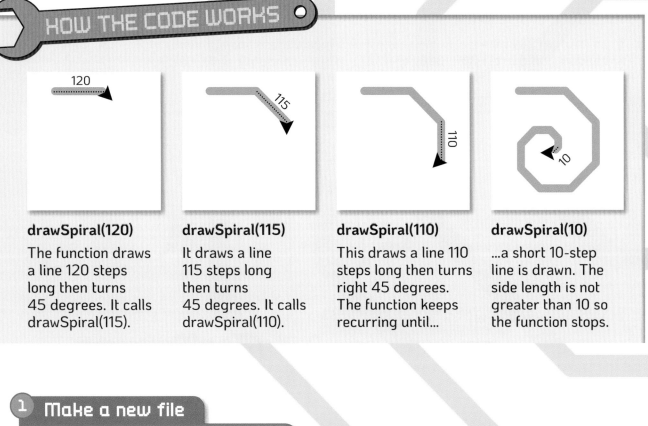

drawSpiral(120)

The function draws a line 120 steps long then turns 45 degrees. It calls drawSpiral(115).

drawSpiral(115)

It draws a line 115 steps long then turns 45 degrees. It calls drawSpiral(110).

drawSpiral(110)

This draws a line 110 steps long then turns right 45 degrees. The function keeps recurring until...

drawSpiral(10)

...a short 10-step line is drawn. The side length is not greater than 10 so the function stops.

1 Make a new file

Start up **IDLE** or click **File** > **New File**.

File   Edit
New File

2 Show line numbers

Click **Options** > **Show Line Numbers**.

Options   Window
Show Code Context
Show Line Numbers

Start coding!

Type in this code:

Keep an eye on the indentation in this code. It needs to be perfect!

```
1 import turtle
2
3 def drawSpiral(side):
4     turtle.fd(side)
5     turtle.rt(45)
6     if(side>10):
7         drawSpiral(side-5)
8
9 turtle.color('orange')
10 turtle.width(5)
11
12 drawSpiral(120)
```

— *Import the graphics library.*

— *Define the **drawSpiral** function.*
— *Draw a line, as long as the value of the **side** variable.*
— *Turn right 45 degrees.*
— *If the value of the **side** variable is greater than 10 then:*
— *Run the function again, with a shorter side length.*

— *Pick the orange colour.*
— *Set the width of the line drawn.*

— *Draw a spiral, starting with a side length of 120.*

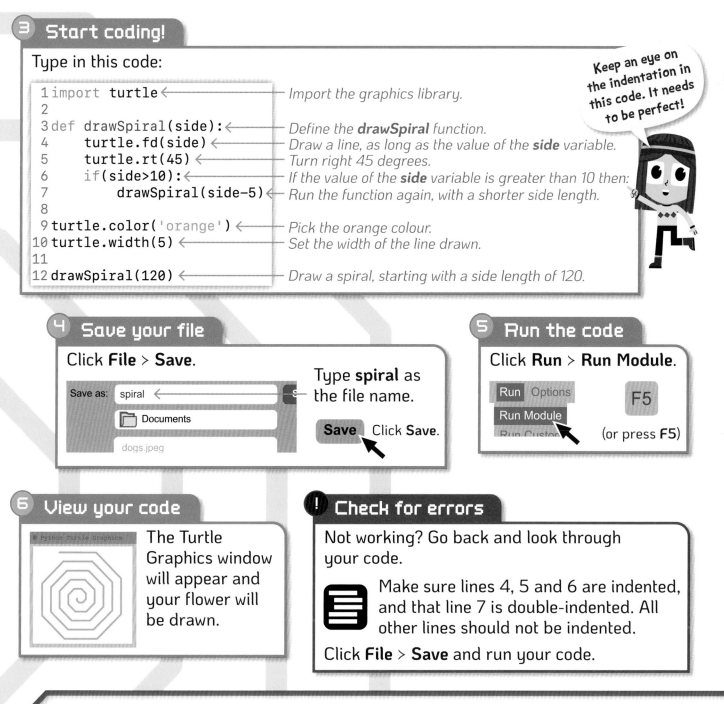

4 Save your file

Click **File** > **Save**.

Save as:	spiral
	Documents
	dogs.jpeg

Type **spiral** as the file name.

Save Click **Save**.

5 Run the code

Click **Run** > **Run Module**.

Run Options
Run Module
Run Custom

F5

(or press **F5**)

6 View your code

The Turtle Graphics window will appear and your flower will be drawn.

Check for errors

Not working? Go back and look through your code.

Make sure lines 4, 5 and 6 are indented, and that line 7 is double-indented. All other lines should not be indented.

Click **File** > **Save** and run your code.

Challenges

Change line 12 to draw different-sized spirals. Change their colour and line thickness.

What happens if you turn by a different angle in line 5 or use a bigger number in line 7?

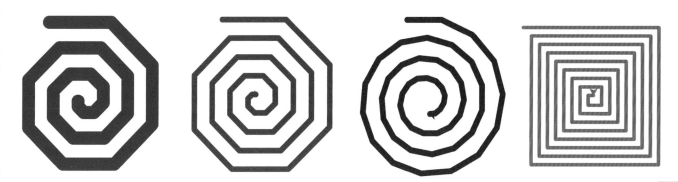

Recursive Squares

The pattern in this project is created by drawing a number of different coloured squares. A recursive function is used to make each square slightly smaller than the previous one and to position it correctly. The function also swaps the colour each time a square is drawn. Once the square gets small, fewer than 20 steps, the function stops.

HOW THE CODE WORKS

Let's see what happens if we start our pattern with a blue square, 80 pixels wide.

```
drawSquare(0,0,80,'blue')
```

1
80

drawSquare(0,0,80,'blue')
This function draws a blue square, 80 pixels wide. It calls drawSquare(10,10,60,'yellow').

2
60

drawSquare(10,10,60,'yellow')
This moves the turtle to (10,10), then draws a yellow square, 60 pixels wide. It calls drawSquare(20,20,40,'blue').

3
40

drawSquare(20,20,40,'blue')
This moves the turtle to (20,20), then draws a blue square 40 pixels wide. It calls drawSquare(30,30,40,'yellow').

4
20

drawSquare(30,30,20,'yellow')
The turtle moves to (30,30) then draws a yellow square, 20 pixels wide. The width is not greater than 20, so no more squares are drawn.

---

1 Make a new Python file

Launch **IDLE** or click **File > New File**.

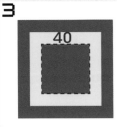

File   Edit
New File

2 Show line numbers

Click **Options > Show Line Numbers**.

Options   Window
Show Code Context
Show Line Numbers

Check the indentation for each line of your code is correct.

3 Start coding!

Type in the code below to run this project:

```
 1 import turtle
 2 turtle.speed(0)
 3
 4 def drawSquare(x,y,w,col):
 5     turtle.goto(x,y)
 6     turtle.color(col,col)
 7     turtle.begin_fill()
 8     for n in range(4):
 9         turtle.fd(w)
10         turtle.rt(90)
11     turtle.end_fill()
12     if(col=='blue'):
13         col='yellow'
14     else:
15         col='blue'
16     if(w>20):
17         drawSquare(x+10,y-10,w-20,col)
18
19 drawSquare(0,0,200,'blue')
```

- 1: *Import the graphics commands.*
- 2: *Set the turtle speed to fast.*
- 4: *Start defining the function to draw the squares.*
- 5: *Move to the coordinates (x,y).*
- 6: *Set the line and fill colour to the value stored in **col**.*
- 7: *Fill the next shape drawn.*
- 8: *Repeat the following indented lines four times:*
- 9: *Draw a line, the length of the variable **w**.*
- 10: *Turn the turtle right 90 degrees.*
- 11: *Fill in the shape that has been drawn.*
- 12: *If the colour stored in the variable **col** is blue...*
- 13: *...then change it to yellow.*
- 14: *If it is not...*
- 15: *...change it to blue.*
- 16: *If the variable **w** is bigger than 20 then:*
- 17: *Draw another square, 10 pixels further along and 20 pixels smaller.*
- 19: *This line calls the function and starts the drawing.*

4 Save your file

Click **File** > **Save**.

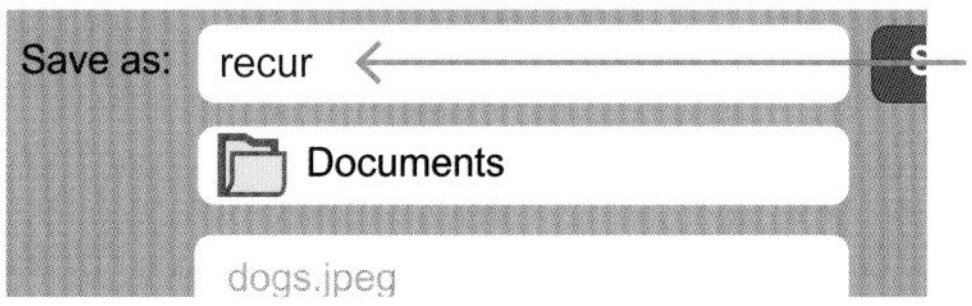
Save as:
recur
Documents
dogs.jpeg

Type **recur** as the file name.

Save

Click **Save**.

5 Run the code

Click **Run** > **Run Module**.

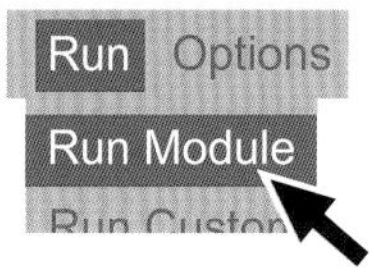
Run
Options
Run Module

F5

(or press **F5**)

6 Squares!

A square pattern like this should be drawn on your screen:

Python Turtle Graphics

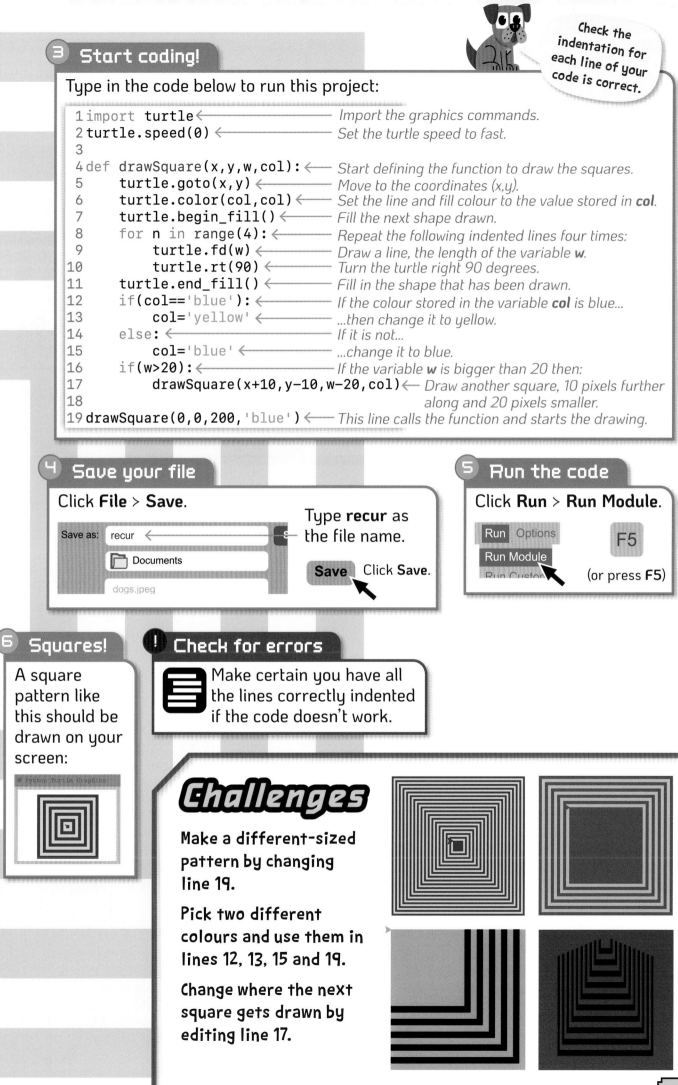

! Check for errors

Make certain you have all the lines correctly indented if the code doesn't work.

Challenges

Make a different-sized pattern by changing line 19.

Pick two different colours and use them in lines 12, 13, 15 and 19.

Change where the next square gets drawn by editing line 17.

Recursive Tree

Recursive patterns can be found in nature. This project uses recursion to draw a tree. We will define a function that draws a branch of a tree. At the end of the branch, the function will call itself again. Each time the function gets called, it will tell Python to make a smaller branch in a different direction. We will use random numbers to make the tree look more realistic.

HOW THE CODE WORKS

Our drawBranch function will use these values.

How long it will be in pixels.
↓

```
drawBranch(x,y,size,deg)
```

Where to start drawing the branch.

The angle it will be pointing (in degrees).

The function starts by drawing the tree trunk (actually, a branch going up).

After the trunk is drawn, the function calls itself to draw two more slightly smaller branches at the end of the trunk.

Two more branches are drawn at the end of each of the first two. The random command makes each branch slightly different.

Another two branches get added at the end of each branch. Because they have got quite small, the function stops.

1 Make a new file

Start up **IDLE** or click **File > New File**.

| File | Edit |
| New File | |

2 Show line numbers

Click **Options > Show Line Numbers**.

Options	Window
Show Code Context	
Show Line Numbers	

Start coding!

Type in this code to draw the tree:

```
1 import turtle                              Import the turtle graphics commands.
2 import random                              Import the random commands.
3
4 def drawBranch(x,y,size,deg):              Define the function to draw a branch.
5     turtle.pu()                            Stop the turtle drawing as it moves.
6     turtle.goto(x,y)                       Move the turtle to the coordinates (x,y).
7     turtle.setheading(deg)                 Point it in the direction stored in the deg parameter.
8     turtle.pd()                            Get the turtle ready to draw.
9     turtle.fd(size)                        Move forward the number of steps set in size.
10    x1=turtle.xcor()                       Find the current x value and store it in x1.
11    y1=turtle.ycor()                       Get the current y value and store it in y1.
12    if(size>5):                            If the size of the branch is bigger than 5, then:
13        ang1=deg-random.randint(15,25)     Pick a random angle for a branch going left.
14        ang2=deg+random.randint(15,25)     Pick a random value for a branch going right.
15        size1=size*random.uniform(0.4,0.8) Choose a random size for the left branch.
16        size2=size*random.uniform(0.4,0.8) Pick a random size for the right branch.
17        drawBranch(x1,y1,size1,ang1)       Call the function to draw the left branch.
18        drawBranch(x1,y1,size2,ang2)       Call the function to draw the right branch.
19
20 turtle.speed(0)                           Set the turtle to draw quickly.
21 drawBranch(0,0,100,90)                    Start drawing the tree with a branch 100 pixels long, pointing up.
```

> The values given to a function (inside the brackets) are called its **parameters**.

④ Save your file

Click **File** > **Save**.

Save as: tree

📁 Documents

dogs.jpeg

Type **tree** as the file name.

Save Click **Save**.

⑤ Run the code

Click **Run** > **Run Module**.

Run Options
Run Module
Run Custom

F5

(or press **F5**)

⑥ View your code

The Turtle Graphics window will start up. Your tree will be drawn, one branch at a time.

⚠ Not working?

Check all the lines are indented correctly. Any mistakes here will stop your code working.

( ) ***** Make sure all the calculations in lines 13 to 16 are typed correctly.

> Experiment with the code so far. Can you change the height of the tree?

Now, add a loop to draw a whole forest of trees!

7 Edit your tree code

Add some more trees by editing the end of your code so that it looks like this:

```
20 turtle.speed(0)          ←———— Make the turtle work fast.
21 for t in range(5):       ←———— Repeat the code below five times.
22     x=200*t-400          ←———— Set the position of the next tree in a variable called x.
23     drawBranch(x,-100,100,90) ←— Start the next tree by drawing a trunk.
```

8 Save and run

Click **File** > **Save**.   Click **F5**.

File Edit
Save

F5

9 View your code

© Python Turtle Graphics

Your forest will start growing in the Turtle Graphics window.

10 Add colour and thickness

Click at the beginning of line 8 and press **Enter** twice. Add these **extra** lines of code:

```
8      turtle.color('brown')    ←———— Set the colour of the tree branch.
9      turtle.width(size*0.08)  ←———— Set the thickness of each branch.
```

This will make the branches thinner as they get shorter.

11 Add leaves

Click at the end of line 20 and press **Enter**. Add these **extra** lines of code:

```
20         drawBranch(x1,y1,size2,ang2)
21     else:←——————————————————————————— Else if the size is 5 or smaller, then:
22         turtle.colormode(255)←———————— Set the colour mode.
23         turtle.color(0,random.randint(50,200),0)←— Pick a random shade of green.
24         turtle.dot(4)←———————————————— Draw a leaf.
```

Make sure the else command is indented in line with the if command in line 12.

12 Save and run

Click **File** > **Save**.   Click **F5**.

File Edit
Save

F5

13 View your code

© Python Turtle Graphics

Challenges

Add more trees.

Add code to make them all random heights.

The trees will now be redrawn with leaves.

Extra challenges

When you have finished the projects in the book, try some of these extra challenges!

Random triple dots

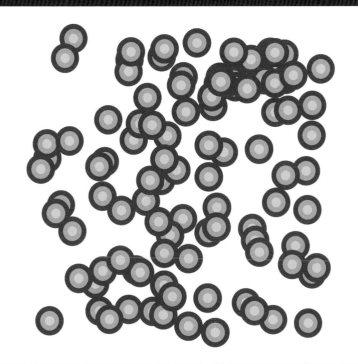

1. Start with the random colours code from page 22.

2. Add a **turtle.penup()** command.

3. Instead of drawing a black dot, change your code so it draws three different-coloured dots. Each dot needs to get smaller – a bit like a small version of the code on page 6.

Experiment with the colour and size of the dots.

Hexagon pattern

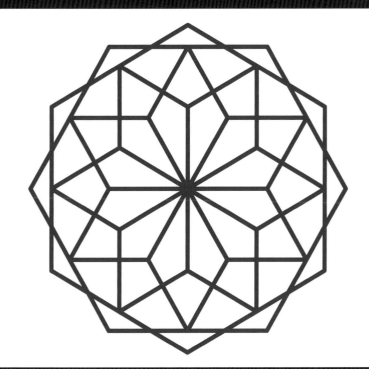

1. Type in the code for the square pattern on pages 12-13.

2. We need to adapt the code so that it draws hexagons instead of squares.

3. Change the loop on line 8 so that it repeats six times – as there are six sides on a hexagon.

4. Change the angle on line 10 from 90 to 60. This is because:
$360 \div 4 = 90$
$360 \div 6 = 60$

5. Can you make a pattern using an octagon?

Random Squares

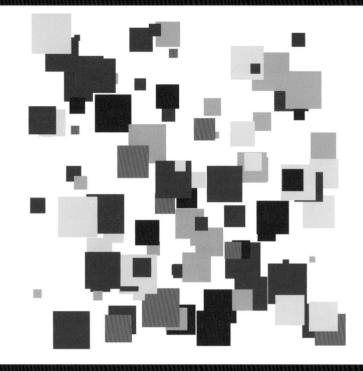

1. Create a function that draws a square. See Step 3 on page 69 for help with that.

2. Make a list called **col** that contains all the colours you want to use.

3. Create a loop that will draw 100 squares. Give each one a random x and y value and a random size and colour. See Step 3 on page 65 for help with that.

> If you complete this challenge, try doing it with another shape – maybe hexagons?

RGB hoops

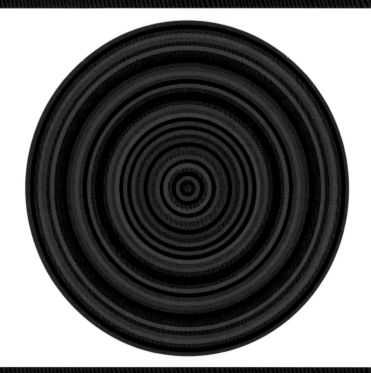

1. Find the code on page 33 that draws random coloured hoops. It uses a list of four colours to make the pattern. Adapt the code so that it picks a random colour using the RGB system.

2. Add a line to set the **colormode** to 255.

3. Use the code at the bottom of page 35 to pick random numbers for R, G and B. Use these values to set the colour.

4. Experiment by setting some of these values to 0 instead and see what happens.

Rabbit

Grrrr!

Look at the code to draw a dog's head on page 59.

Sketch a simple rabbit's head on a piece of paper. Work out which parts will be similar to the dog, and which parts will be different. For example, the ears will need to go upwards instead of downwards.

Adapt the dog code to draw your rabbit.

Squared paper is great for planning pictures like this.

Coloured dot grid

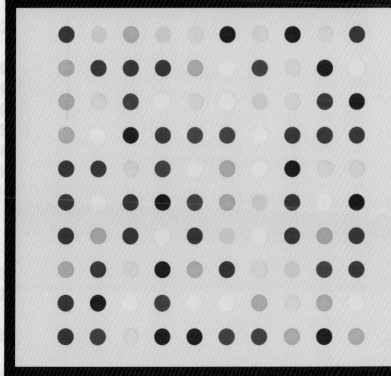

1. Make a **for x in range** loop. It should run from –300 to 300 in steps of 60.

2. Make a **for y in range** loop with the same values.

```
for x in range(-300,300,60):
    for y in range(-300,300,60):
```

Add some code to draw a random coloured dot at the coordinates (x,y). See page 24 for help with setting random colours from a list.

Blended stars

1. Type in the Colour mix points code from page 42.

2. Delete the command that draws a dot on line 13.

3. Delete the **pu (penup)** command. You may need to add it in later somewhere else.

4. Add some code to draw a star.

```
for s in range(5):
    turtle.fd(50)
    turtle.rt(144)
```

I'm seeing stars!

Combined picture

1. Combine together the code from several projects to make a picture.

2. Start by setting a background colour, then bring in some trees from the project on pages 72–74.

3. Add a **square** function (from page 64) and draw a large green square very low down to make the grass. It can overlap the bottom of the trees.

4. Add the code to draw some flowers from page 67. You will need to change the code to make the flowers smaller.

5. Add any ideas of your own!

COPY AND PASTE CODE

You can combine code from different projects by using copy and paste:

Highlight code from one project.

Click **Edit** > **Copy**.

Go to the new project and position the cursor.

Click **Edit** > **Paste**.

Python commands

PYTHON CODE	MEANING
`import turtle`	Load the code in the turtle graphics module.
`for n in range(4):`	Repeat a block of code four times.
`def`	Define a function.
`if`	Run a block of code if something is true.
`else`	Run a different block of code if it is false.
`x=5`	Create a variable called **x** with a value of 5.
`col=['red','blue']`	Make a list called **col** with two items in it.

TURTLE MODULE CODE	MEANING
`turtle.back(30)` *(or bk)*	Move the turtle back 30 pixels.
`turtle.begin_fill()`	Fill any graphics that are drawn after this command.
`turtle.bgcolor('red')`	Set the background colour to red.
`turtle.color('red')`	Set the turtle's colour to red.
`turtle.color(255,0,0)`	Set the turtle's colour using RGB values.
`turtle.colormode(255)`	Set the colour mode for the turtle.
`turtle.dot(50)`	Draw a dot 50 pixels wide.
`turtle.end_fill()`	Fill any graphics drawn since the **begin_fill** command.
`turtle.forward(50)` *(or fd)*	Move the turtle forward 50 pixels.
`turtle.goto(50,30)`	Move the turtle to the coordinates (50,30).
`turtle.left(90)` *(or lt)*	Rotate the turtle 90 degrees to the left.
`turtle.pendown()` *(or pd)*	Put the pen down to start the turtle drawing.
`turtle.penup()` *(or pu)*	Lift the pen up to stop the turtle drawing.
`turtle.setheading(45)` *(or seth)*	Point the turtle in the direction 45 degrees.
`turtle.speed(0)`	Tell the turtle to move quickly.
`turtle.width(20)`	Make the turtle's line 20 pixels wide.

RANDOM MODULE CODE	MEANING
`random.randint(1,6)`	Pick a random integer (whole number) between 1 and 6.
`random.uniform(0.5,1.5)`	Pick a random number between 0.5 and 1.5.
`random.choice(col)`	Pick an item at random from the list called col.

Glossary

Algorithm A set of rules or steps to make a game or program work.

Argument The value passed to a function when it is called.

Bug A mistake or error in a program that stops it running correctly.

Code A series of commands or instructions.

Command An instruction or piece of code that tells the computer to do something.

Coordinates The position of an image on the screen, set by x and y values.

Function One or more lines of code combined together to carry out a particular task.

IDLE Interactive Development and Learning Environment. The program that is used to write and run Python code on a computer.

Indent Spaces at the start of a line of Python code. Used to show where a block of code starts and finishes.

Library Often used to describe a module, but could actually be multiple modules.

Loop A block or section of code that is repeated over and over again.

Module A file containing functions that can be used within Python to give it extra commands.

Nested A loop that runs inside another loop.

Output The text or graphics that are shown by Python when some code is run.

Parameter The value inside a function definition — similar to an argument.

Pixel One of the millions of tiny dots on a computer screen, combined together to show text, graphics or videos.

Procedure Another name for a function.

Random A number that cannot be guessed or predicted.

Recursion When a function calls itself over and over again until something happens.

Syntax The way words and symbols are arranged to make code.

Text editor A program used to type code in.

Turtle An image that moves around, drawing on the screen when commands are given.

Variable A number or piece of information that can change while a program is running, such as the score in a game.